D1266587

UNITY THROUGH LOVE

UNITY THROUGH LOVE

Essays in Ecumenism

JEAN GUITTON

HERDER AND HERDER

1964
HERDER AND HERDER, NEW YORK
232 Madison Avenue, New York 16, N.Y.

Translated from *Vers l'unite dans l'amour* (Grasset, Paris) by Brian Thompson.

Nihil obstat: Patrick A. Barry
Censor Librorum

Imprimatur: ✠Robert F. Joyce
Bishop of Burlington
August 8, 1964

The nihil obstat and imprimatur are official declarations that a book or pamphlet is free of doctrinal or moral error. No implication is contained therein that those who have granted the nihil obstat and imprimatur agree with the contents, opinions or statements expressed.

Library of Congress Catalog Card Number: 64–19728

Printed in the United States of America

CONTENTS

Preface

The idea which inspires this work is easy to express: true unity does not reduce to nothing the persons or the communities which it brings together. True unity permits each of the beings, until now separated (thus imperfect, and thereby unhappy), to be to a greater extent itself.

The word "love"—so vague, so ambiguous—could here receive an exact and legitimate meaning. I call "love" that higher, more profound and purer existence which makes it possible to unite oneself to another being (be it a person, a communion of persons or, at the limit, the absolute Author of beings) in an exchange of fullness in which one gives everything in order to receive everything. One is all the more united to others as one casts off that which was exclusive in one's attachment to oneself and, inversely, all the more oneself as one has given oneself to the other.

This search for Unity through the diversity of natures and gifts characterizes supreme efforts: those of the philosopher when he attempts to understand the laws of being; those of the statesman when he works for the good of the social body; those of the artist when he does the work of a creator with an indifferent, incoherent material, which he must unite, yet not unify; those of the man who builds his destiny by trying to make likes, tendencies and accidents concur.

I remember having heard the philosopher Emile Boutroux in 1921, the last year of his life. Gustave Lanson had asked him to come to the École Normale, before several students of philosophy, to hand over to us his experience. In the end, it was a testament. The tall, pale old man quoted to us, as summing up the interrogation and the solution of a life of research, these two maxims, one from a Greek sage, the other from Pascal.

The first is: πῶς δὲ μοι ἕν τι τὰ πάντ' ἔσται χαὶ χωρὶς ἕχαστον: What must be done, that for me the whole be in some way one and that each part of the whole be nonetheless itself apart?

And here is the thought of Pascal: "All is one, the one is in the other, like the Three Persons."

That was the time when, under the impulse of Père Portal, I was awakening to the ecumenical spirit. In a recent book of reminiscences, *Dialogue avec les Précurseurs,*[1] I told of the circumstances, the conjunctures. Here, it is the ideas which will have precedence over the images.

For my mind infatuated with synthesis and analogy, there was no radical difference between metaphysical exercise and ecumenical effort. In the light of these thoughts, I realized that unity always works upon Being, though it be in a different way in each case. The work of the Church

[1] Paris (Aubier).

did not seem to me separated from the operation of being. It is always a question of uniting without confusing, of distinguishing without separating—and that in a nuclear, delicate, unfathomable and detailed labor—far more difficult, real and efficacious than the syntheses in triad, drawn from Hegel, which our century honors so highly under the ancient name of "dialectics."

One could even say that the true dialectics, in this moment of history, is the Church's work for visible unity. Yes, such is perhaps one of the most efficacious means of inserting some *freedom* into "becoming." One can ask oneself, from the point of view of the faith, if the confused desire of modern men does not translate obscurely a certain unacknowledged haunting memory of the mystery of the incarnation.

The diverse chapters of this work were written at different dates, in very different circumstances. The thoughts which animate each of these chapters are not linked like the diverse moments of a progression. They digress each time, starting from a new runway, linked by their aspiration toward one and the same end: they converge toward one and the same Center.

But just as our thoughts—though independent of the moment, of the place, of the circumstance—find themselves rooted, I am going to precede this work, happily delayed, with a fragment from my *Journal.*

At Rome

October 11, 1962

I regret that the French language does not possess an adjective to indicate that a being is "unique of its kind." This adjective would be quite necessary for those who were present at this sublime morning. The television viewers probably saw almost everything from several perspectives: for several hours they were endowed with the ubiquity of the angels. But he who was there, incarnate in the discomfort and the density of presence, who enjoyed the colors, so iridescent in the vague odor of the incense, he who was there could tell himself that he coincided with the soul of the event, whereas the others received but the image of it. It is two o'clock in the afternoon. St. Peter's is empty. The world has already resumed its pace. Rome is at rest. I ask myself: "*For me, what has just happened?*"

I sum it up in a single word: an extraordinary condensation of space and time, such as I will never meet with again in this life.

Of time, first of all, since in these Roman ceremonies

all of history is present. A society regards itself there in the diverse epochs, the diverse ages which it has passed through, then assumed, and which compose its youth and its wrinkles. In addition to the ancient liturgies which made us go back in time to the first centuries of the Church, when the liturgy was celebrated in the Greek language (on the circus of the Vatican where St. Peter was immolated), there were there images and recollections from the Middle Ages, from the Renaissance, from modern times—all that capped, reflected, multiplied by the cameras which were outlined at every angle, with their forms of unknown insects, of giant and immobile grasshoppers, probably images of the technics to come.

There was also all human space, in the sense that around the old Europe still too preponderant in quantity, Africa, Asia were there.

And one perceived the image and the phantom of the ancient Powers dispossessed, of the kings in exile.

It was a curious thing, under the maternal, indifferent eye of this old Roman Church so accustomed to respects, to deferments of hope and to a solemn indifference, this calm and unperturbed juxtaposition of seeds and debris.

And if ever the universe were to come to an end tomorrow by mistake, this world, so weary and so hopeful, so blasé and so frenzied, would explode after having contemplated this morning at the Vatican the most beautiful self-image that it could give itself, in the noblest of what it has lived through.

I saw the bishops very badly from the place where I was,

but enough to be possessed of a great hope when I saw an enormous, immaculate mitre cover a black head, gleaming and young. I seemed to see Pascal scrawl on a paper a thought of this kind: "*Unity without variety is tyranny, variety without unity is dissension; it is necessary to combine unity and variety and make that which is one, varied, and that which is varied, one.*"

Here I am, so situated that I see scarcely more than three faces. First, beside me, that of my friend Veronese, who has long been the President of UNESCO and here represents culture. Just opposite, on the bench of the observers, who are highly honored, I regard the contemplative visage of Pastor Schutz of Taizé. Between two columns, I perceive the paternal, firm profile, engraved like a medal, of John XXIII. From time to time I hear his voice, firm, strong and musical, which resounds like a bell of hope, while Cardinal Tisserant, with a typically French accent, chants the Mass. One would think oneself in a village of Lorraine, at Domrémy, during the Solemn Mass.

Struck by the prayerful, wholly spiritual attitude of the representatives of India and Africa, no matter what their attire, it seems to me that the white race is less penetrated by the spirit in its very body than this Orient, which has not yet fully assimilated Christianity.

Contrary to so many ceremonies which are more boring the longer they last, this one, though slow and long, was ceaselessly renewed, and the interest of it, as it were, increased. (The only thing that I regret is not having seen any young faces. The totality of the participants was on the downward slope of life.) After the procession, after the obedience—which permits a contact from heart to heart of the Pope with the cardinals, and which is touching in that—after the supplication in Eastern rite, what was for me the most moving was to listen to the address of the Pope, spoken with a voice firm, joyous and elastic like his gait, and which was of a wonderful fullness of meaning. As he spoke, I translated what I am going to cite: "This being well established, one sees clearly what must be expected from the council with respect to doctrine. The twenty-first ecumenical council, which will benefit from an extremely useful and considerable sum of experiences in the juridical, apostolic and administrative domains, wants to transmit the doctrine in its purity and integrity, exempt from weakenings and alterations—the doctrine which during twenty centuries, despite difficulties and oppositions, has become a common patrimony for men. A patrimony which all do not accept willingly, and nevertheless a wealth always offered to men of good will.

"Our duty is not only to guard this precious treasure as if we had concern but for the past, but to give ourselves, with a resolute will and without any fear, to the work which our age demands, thus following the path which the Church has been traveling for twenty centuries.

"The essential object of this council is therefore not a discussion on this or that article of the fundamental doctrine of the Church, a discussion which would largely take up again the teaching of the Fathers and of ancient and modern theologians; this teaching is always supposed fairly present and familiar to minds.

"For such a resumption there was no need of a council. But from the renewed adhesion, in serenity and in calm, to the whole teaching of the Church in its plenitude and its precision, such as it continues to shine in the conciliar acts of Trent and Vatican I, the Christian, apostolic and Catholic spirit in the entire world awaits a distinct advance in the sense of the penetration of the doctrine and the formation of consciences, in more perfect correspondence with the professed fidelity to the authentic doctrine—this doctrine being, moreover, studied and set forth according to the methods of research and the presentation used by modern thought. The substance of the ancient doctrine contained in the deposit of faith is one thing, the formulation in which it is couched, being regulated in regard to forms and proportions by the needs of a ministry and of a style above all pastoral, is another."

The Pope, who seemed a little fatigued at the beginning of the ceremony, took on vigor and force as time went on, and he concluded this image with a voice both stronger and more tender at the same time: "*The council which is beginning is a day of light. It is now barely dawn, and already the first announcement of the day fills my heart with such tenderness. We contemplate the stars whose brightness adds to the majesty of this time. Now, you yourselves are these stars.*"

At this moment (I do not know if the television viewers

noticed it), one saw that certain bishops looked first of all toward the sky. Then, embarrassed to know that the stars were they themselves, they brought their glances back to the visages of the other bishops who were placed opposite them.

It had rained a great deal last night. And this morning still when we took our places in the nave. But the sun had risen. And this progression of the light from the storm to this mild October noon seems a mysterious approval.

PART ONE

THE THOUGHT

1 The Council

1
The Council and the Crisis of Humanity

The temporal world is regulated and unfolds according to the law of rhythms. And although the evolution of the historic universe takes place on a single axis, one observes periods which succeed one another like waves on the ocean of the ages.

And each time a rhythm declines and is about to come to an end (to resume tomorrow in another amplitude and in unforeseeable modes), each time a period is in the process of abating, one witnesses a phenomenon of aging, of fall and of decadence. Then there are atmospheres of life and of thought which become rarefied; there are techniques which live on, which tomorrow will be forever outmoded; there are powers which no longer have anything but the appearance. And, under the same décor which believes itself eternal and is enchanted by its last rays, there are new seeds, inventions, new departures. One cannot write true history, which is integral history, that which was formerly called "universal history," history on *the highest scale* (and thus the closest to the creative regard), without applying oneself to describing the rhythms of different amplitude, which are situated at different levels of depth, which overlap one another, but whose complex and varied development constitutes the fabric and splendor of history, and makes it similar, St. Augustine said, to music *quasi magnum carmen ineffabilis modulatoris.*

Now, the character of the present era and what makes it so incomprehensible to those who live in it, is the fact that several historic rhythms, independent from one another, happen to present *at the same time* a decadent phase.

This coincidence of *nodes* (to speak the language of vibratory movements) is very improbable. It is what gives our era an eschatological character. One is inclined to wonder if the end of time cannot be exactly defined: *the convergence of all decadences.*

Which are these historic rhythms that, in our era, mark a time of retreat, that advance toward the end or the transmutation?

2
When Three Ages Come to an End Together

❨ 1

I consider first a technical phenomenon of very great amplitude: the end of the period which begins with the appearance of the human phenomenon and in which the energy tapped and utilized was borrowed from superficial and, so to speak, extrinsic layers of matter: be it the energy of animal muscle, that of waters and winds, that of steam and its elastic expansion, or that of explosion and of electricity. Nothing can compare with the intra-atomic energy which is linked to the substance, to the consistency of matter itself. We are entering into a new age, so new that the analogies of the past no longer help us.

Here we have come to the end also of that period, dating from the origins, in which humanity was not yet favored with a central nervous system. It was broken up into closed groups, distant in space and not living in the same duration. One sees the time coming (and it has, in certain points, already come) when events, through their images, will be present everywhere at once, when there will no longer be any *local* crisis, when conditions will be ready for a single world state, a planetary empire.

But one can observe rhythms of lesser amplitude, restrict one's regard to the history of Christianity.

2

Several critics have noted that one has seen decrease, decline, even cessation in more than one case, that phase of the life of the Church which had begun with the conversion of the Emperor Constantine, and which one sometimes calls "the Constantinian age."

It is the phase of the history of the Church in which the Christians cease being hidden in the furrows of the world, like accursed seeds, without honor, without visibility, without security of life and of possession, without participating in structures and in culture . . . to see themselves suddenly thrown into honor and light. Henceforth everything is changed. The empire outwardly protects the Christians; the Emperor presides over the councils. The civilization becomes little by little Christian. The papacy comes into the heritage of the western empire. . . . And, for many minds, civilization, culture, power, career on the one hand, and faith, Christian fidelity, labor for the Church on the other, are very closely related terms. This state of affairs, which so aided the faith to penetrate the manners, the institutions, to incarnate Christianity in the cities, to give a terrestrial visage to the city of God, is tending to cease. Nowadays one observes a gap between the faith and its temporal supports.

Henceforth one sees the image which one has formed till now of several Catholic institutions changing. The most striking example is that of the temporal power of the popes. In our era, the papacy no longer appears to have need of a state to support it. Napoleon had himself "consecrated": nowadays, what power would think of a consecration? —Likewise, the problem of the missions is changing profoundly in consequence of the shrinking of distances, of the solidarity (material and spiritual) of the diverse parts of the world. All nations have been "evangelized," in the sense that they have received Christian missionaries. But all the same, the universe has not listened to them. Outwardly more educated, it believes itself henceforth capable of refuting them.

Newman foresaw an era in which the great majority of men would say to the missionaries: "What you preach to us has been refuted, we don't have to refute it again." For our modern missionaries, and increasingly so, it will not be a candid ignorance to be educated, but a well-informed negation which they will have to meet face to face: the reconquest will demand methods other than those of the conquest. Then, since great portions of the earth received the Gospel on the occasion of the implantation of the technically superior white race, Christianity has suffered from being confused with the West and its power. The culture, in several countries, has become purely secular, indifferent to religion. In other countries, the Church is muzzled. Humanity believes that it is arriving at an adult age by the very fact that it is liberating itself from the Church and from what conveyed it.

Here again, we are penetrating into a new age, a difficult age, which we dread to see dawn; to navigate on this black ocean, we have received neither boat nor sail.

❡ 3

A third rhythm, more difficult to discern, is the rhythm of the Catholic faith in western, evangelized consciences. Here again, we are arriving at the end of an age: the age in which the Christian faith, defined by the formulas of the first ecumenical councils, was shared by the totality of the faithful, despite several rending separations. This quartering had not shattered the body of the faith which, in the depths of assent, remained a common property, virtually possessed, despite the scission of schism and the fission of heresy.

Today, it is impossible for a dispute about the incarnation, about grace or even about the nature of the Church to bring about social phenomena of historically visible separation, influencing the general course of political events. In one sense, we are at the end of *the age of heresies* of a dogmatic type, an age which began very early with Docetism and Gnosticism, and which presented remarkable apogees in the fourth century with Arius and in the sixteenth century with Luther. This growing insensibility of the peoples to the problems posed by the faith was already visible at the time of Vatican I: and it is precisely to face up to it that that council had been convened, under the lucid impulse of Pius IX. One must not believe that as a consequence of this dogmatic indifference humanity has ceased becoming impassioned and divided in the search for the absolute. If Vatican Council I did not find before it dogmatic errors to condemn (like the Council of Trent), it was not because the faith of evangelized humanity was stronger or more unanimous. Certainly not! It was because the constant and extremely cunning adversary of the Christian name was making his attacks *at the level still more profound than the assent to the dogmas and facts of Christianity;* I mean: on the plane of the essential bases and roots and substructures, on the plane of the philosophical truths implied in the faith, and which are its condition of emergence and of life, truths of morality and religion formerly called "natural morality" and "natural religion" in the sense that they are the common bond of men—in a word: on the plane of the *foundations.* In contemporary society, and in all climates, the negation of God became a learned negation, based *in appearance* on experience, confirmed *according to appearances* by the successes of technics. This negation penetrated that unconscious of the peoples and the masses which is the reservoir of beliefs. Nowadays a would-be rational, scientific, humanist atheism is taught by the empires, supported by the technics of celestial successes; the nonfaith in God possesses virtually a third of the human race. And tomorrow it will probably be half. That has never been seen since the origin of this thinking species. For the Mediterranean paganisms, the African animisms, and even the Indian or Chinese pantheisms and the European secularisms still contained a divine affirmation and the sense of a certain mystery. The idea of the divine, of the invisible, of the sacred was a common possession of humanity which had never denied the beyond.

Let us examine more closely how this radical conflict appears at the present time—this conflict which opposes two spiritual races within one and the same humanity and which represents the most insidious danger that the religion of Abraham and of Jesus (even, indeed, that of Mohammed, which keeps the monotheism of Israel) has known.

As far back as the Renaissance, one could discern a separation between the mental universe of man and the mental universe of the Christian. For ten centuries, it had been almost the same thing to think as a man and to think as a Christian! The two universes coincided: it was the extremely beautiful unity of Christian civilization, symbolized in the systematics of the *Summa Theologica* and the architecture of the cathedrals. Nowadays it is becoming difficult for some minds, impossible practically, to think of themselves as men of science and to think of themselves at the same time as men of faith.

It is the plague of *homo modernus* to bear within him this division!

And, when this *homo modernus* is a believer, this wound is still present. For many educated believers live on two levels. The laboratory does not communicate with the chapel. And when, by some stroke of luck, the teachings of science and those of the faith resemble one another, they appear to be "concordant." But those words "concordance," "concordat," even "concord," dear to the nineteenth century, are ambiguous words. They divert the suspicion of a too visible rivalry. But they do not signify real agreement, hidden, constant and true harmony. Political power often asphyxiates a religion it no longer persecutes: for it is much more rewarding not to attack it and to be content with ignoring it. Silence kills better than the sword. Such is the character of this end of the third rhythm.

Everything is taking place as if the conditions were ready for a Religion of Science and Technics to grow and impose itself, an adoration without worship transferred from the known God to the unknown god for matter, of evolution, of life, of the cosmos, of humanity, of organizing thought, technical or political. In a word, let us say: *A Religion of the World*, not of the *beyond* but of what is *on this side*, an "anthropocosmics" whose dogma would be a *cosmogenesis*. And that which we call Marxism, communism, atheism, humanism, rationalism does not mean anything else. These are just so many effects of a more profound cause; which is the end of what I have called the age of heresies, the first period of the rhythm of the faith.

One could probably find several other rhythms which are waning and declining, but they remain secondary in relation to those which I envisage.[1]

It seems that these diverse rhythms, independent from one another, under the effect of one and the same overstepping, as if they felt that they are going toward one and the same point of metamorphosis, have an action upon one another . . . It is the feeling of their convergence which gives to some the impression that humanity is heading toward a crisis, toward a final period which would not be merely "the end of a time" but "the end *of time*."

3
The Council Facing the Three Present Crises

It is in perspectives perhaps too high for our limited vision that one can attempt to situate the work of the council.

John XXIII often indicated that the council would have a twofold aspect, a twofold influence: one which re-

[1] Thus the rhythm of the transmission of knowledge by writing alone seems to have to make room for a new rhythm in which, by the image immediately broadcast, the human mind, without the intervention of language and words, will be placed in the presence of the thing itself.

mains interior to the Catholic Church, which he calls "religious"—the other exterior, which he calls "social." I want to retain above all this latter action, since I envisage very general rhythms of human history.

I divide my meditation into three levels, corresponding to each of the nodes previously defined.

¶ 1

How is the council going to face up to this beginning of a new technical age: the atomic age? It is clear that the Church has nothing to say about atomic technology as such: the Church does not condemn science, she encourages it in its researches, because science and technics work to make man capable of participating in the creative force. But the Church can act in order to keep man from being destroyed by his progress.

How?

By giving to humanity full consciousness of its real unity, by hindering it, therefore, from meeting face to face in two factions which would wage an inexpiable war. For the Church is practically the only universal society, *really instituted and organic*, in which all nations cooperate without hypocrisy, and that for twenty centuries. She can constitute above the peoples and the nations a real *super-society* of truly spiritual men who, at a moment of crisis, would place themselves between the factions in conflict. One can conceive a body of reforms, slowly and progressively introduced, which would give the Church a catholicity still more visible and more organic.

By procuring for the Church more and more the visage of a Church of the Poor. And I take the word "Poor" here in the strongest sense. The *appearance* of a propertied Church must cease, above all among her officials, in face of a world ever more dispossessed. In the Marxist universe, the Church is described according to its appearances: twenty million rich whites, the Gospel of the Poor in hand, before a billion poor. It is not a question of criticizing the past, when the Church, to defend its freedom, was obliged to take powers, and with these powers colors, habits, advantages. But the *princes of this world* are no longer the kings, nor even the "bourgeoise." They are the disinherited, organized into states which are their emanations, which even possess certain technical superiorities. And the reason which made the Church desire a "temporal power" to be able to control the temporal forces should now make her attentive to the inverse necessity, but which is at bottom identical in its principle: that of being ever more the protectress of those who *do not have enough* in the face of the conscious and unconscious injustices of those who *have too much*. John XXIII, born poor, put a great deal of emphasis on this poverty which he wanted to present to the world before the council under the twofold image of the poor house of Nazareth at Loreto and of the Poor One of Assisi.

By recalling to men, with gravity, insistence and solemn precision, with the rigor and the vigor of the Gospel of the apostles, of the councils and of the popes, that there EXISTS a BEING (by whatever name one designates him in societies), the "Creator and Renumerator for those who seek him," as the Epistle to the Hebrews says, the final judge of consciences. That, consequently, technical progress, as great as it may be, the arrangement of the universe, comfort, the destruction of physical pain, the prolongation of life or, moreover, the colonization of the planets, even at the limit the exploration of the entire cosmos—that, which seems to be EVERYTHING, is NOTHING, if this progress makes man forget his relation of dependence with his Creator and his Judge. The importance of such a reminder at this moment of history is such that, if the council limited itself to that, it would have accomplished for humanity that after which "the rest is thrown in for good measure" (Mt 6:33). And the coming diminution of the proportional *quantity* of Catholics in the world (in the year 2000, there will no longer be but *one* in *ten*) would not be very redoubtable, if the Church had only the quality, *which is quantity in its nascent state.*

2

Let us envisage now what the Church of the council can do in regard to the end of the second rhythm, which I have called "Constantinian."

It is clear that, if the Church can and probably should, in several cases, disengage herself from an outmoded structure (be it sacral, imperial, bourgeois, western, Hellenic . . . , or whatever) which, during long periods, has supported and aided her in her transcendent work, it is not in order to reduce herself to an organ of pure Spirit, to a seed without humus, to ferment without leaven, to an inspiration without worship, to a body without hierarchy, to an essence without strength—as if from now on she were giving up being incarnate in historic structures, as if from now on she considered herself a Church of angels.

No, if it is a question for the Church of divesting herself of certain ancient garments, it is not in order to be immediately super-clothed in glory, or reduced to a sort of disincarnate nudity; but it is in order to clothe herself in other structures, still unforeseeable, which will compose the civilization of tomorrow. The idea of rhythm which guides me here is very different from that of Evolution, of Progress or of Dialectic. It implies recommencements. It is possible that humanity is opening, as several have said, into a new Middle Ages. Why wouldn't Evolution take place in a spiral, such that the same rhythms would resume on more and more condensed levels? Wouldn't that be true "Dialectic"?

But here, one can say that the council—by the very fact that it has been convoked and convened, that it is unfolding at Rome facing the world in labor, in the crisis of childbirth—is preparing a superior conversion of humanity and is disposing it to shake off like dust what is outmoded in the past, in order to retain but what is a germ of the future.

The council, in the Church, could take the initiative of a very long, very hard, but very necessary work of discernment.

To discern between that which should cease and slowly

disappear through inanition, because inadequate for the new period into which we are entering, and that which should remain, appear, grow and develop.

It is in this perspective that I foresee the problem of the *Christian* people and of its participation, as strong as formerly but more carefully thought out, in the liturgy, that mysterial life of the Church which joins her time to her eternity.

In the word *laïque* ("lay," "layman"), it is easy to recognize the Greek root, which means people. The Church of tomorrow must no longer appear like a pyramid in which the popular, "lay" base would support the hierarchical and hieratic summits, but on the contrary like a plant whose seed, grading and ordering, sinks itself into the earth, and vivifies the lay blossomings of the faithful.

Several reforms, demanded by the ecclesial conscience of the Second Vatican Council, are going to have the effect of attenuating certain differences, excessive for all appearances, between the "clergy" and the "laity." In several domains, one will make the effort to reproduce that state of the Church in the epistles of St. Paul, in which the differences between apostles, prophets and doctors were more functional divisions (like that of respiration and nutrition in the body) than separations of value and of dignity—it being well understood that direction, control, sovereignty are eminently (like the encephalon) functions necessary to the common good.

It is by going back as to a source (more than as to a model) to her apostolic and post-apostolic period that the Church can, in many countries, preserve her essence—especially in missionary countries or in countries in which she is muzzled. It is also by thinking out this essence disencumbered of contingent and passing veneers that the Church can find herself fit to discover the new accommodations of one and the same substance.

⁋ 3

Let us envisage now "the end of all heresies," that is, the problem of the faith and ecumenism.

I have already said how indispensable it was that Vatican II, extending on this point Vatican I, affirm in broad daylight that common possession of the intelligence already defined by the noblest thinkers of paganism, namely: the existence of God, known by the ways of reason and experience, that of the moral law, of natural justice. Thus, the Church will appear as the authorized spokesman of the most constant human tradition.

But "the end of heresies" is manifested by a new position of the relations between "disunited Christians."

It is not a matter, in any case, of merging the Catholics and the separated Christians into one syncretic society, in which one would agree upon a vague and common minimum, putting the dogmatic differences between parentheses. No one in the churches is thinking at present of this "panchristism."

It is a matter of seeking the elements of a possible dialogue, of bringing to light a certain number of principles admitted on both sides, and which could be not the final point of a mongrel agreement, but the basis of departure for a search of the consequences of doctrine and practice which spring from common beliefs. This method of open, patient and informed research supposes negative conditions. Thus: that one give up rhetorical and polemic usages, caricatures, summary condemnations. That one admit the idea (without specifying the proportions) of a mutual fault in the past. In regard to the positive conditions, the principal one consists in an historical study of the different dogmatic formulations seemingly irreconcilable, in order to discern that which, in this opposition, derives from mentalities now outmoded, from circumstances now different, and that which derives from a fundamental and irreductible difference.

With such methods, which were, as we shall see, those of Leibniz and Newman (of Halifax and Mercier, of Cullmann and Couturier in our time), it is possible to diminish the differences of the Christian confessions. It is possible—and that immediately—to substitute for the defiance in men's hearts the confidence, the hope of *unity at the limit*, although one cannot foresee the day and the mode.

When John XXIII received the "observers" on Saturday, October 13, he told them that the secret maxim of his life was the surrender to God from moment to moment, from day to day, with availability and without wanting to know what the future would be. It is thus that he had been appointed to Paris; that he had been made pope; that he had set the council in motion. That meant: "Regarding the union of Christians, let us not seek to know the hour and the manner. That does not concern any of us." And as for me, how can I help recalling the song of Newman which the Anglican Church has retained among its beautiful hymns: "Lead, Kindly Light, . . . Lead Thou me on! . . . one step enough for me."

Catholics will never make any concessions regarding their essence: the *oneness* of the Church of Peter, "head of speech and of conduct," said Bossuet the Gallican. But, precisely because of that, it is their duty to do everything that is possible in the rectification, in the reduction to the essential. Responsible for unity, they are also and for the same reason responsible for the conditions favorable to unity, *responsible for love*. They would be culpable if they raised in the face of unity a condition which were not essential.

One could not put too much emphasis on the human, worldwide importance, not of the immediate unification of separated Christians (which remains in the domain of the impossible: this field is reserved to God), but of the feeling of a convergence toward unity, henceforth desired by all Christians.

In a sense, it would be the end of the period opened by the great reformers of the sixteenth century. The movement of Luther presented two elements, one of which was *the protest* against Rome, and the other *the reform* of the Church. Now, if the spirit of ecumenism triumphed, the element of protest, although remaining for many secondary aspects, would lose some of its virulence, while the element of reform would alone remain—accepted also by Catholics, who have always admitted that the Church had to purify herself.

❙ 4

We are at a grave hour of the history of humanity and the history of the Church: an hour of exceptional change, in which everything can come to an end, or everything can begin again, in accordance with our hope. Several spiritual thinkers of this time herald, after an extreme crisis, a "Pentecost of Love" in which Christ would become the synthetic bond of a humanity renewed in him.

It would nonetheless be unreasonable to expect a miracle from this council, or even spectacular changes. Nothing lasting comes about thus, by magic. Everything will come about over a length of time and through the help of patience and suffering, from obscure germs, from almost indiscernible seeds.

But, by this council which resembles none of the others, Pope John, happy to bear the name of two precursors, has opened, we believe, a new era in the history of the Church. And he has brought help to fragile human history. This generation will probably not become fully aware of it: it will probably be, once the council is closed, sensible above all to the imperfections. But the next generation, judging this new rhythm and its first developments, will recognize that with Vatican II the Church has grown young again.

2 Christ: Total Synthesis

A synthesis is an *assumption* in which the diverse elements dissociated by analysis, the preparatory groups, the provisional wholes, the separated currents are going to meet again in a higher light and verify that beautiful saying of Leibniz: "Inferior things revive in superior things more noble than in themselves."

If a synthesis is really that: not a *summation,* but an *assumption,* not a juxtaposition but a structure, not an old being but a *creatura nova*—synthesis is probably humanly impossible.

For a Christian, he who is "yesterday, today and forever" (Heb 13:8), he by whom the diversities of this world were founded, in whom they have their link and their consistency, he who, "born before all creatures," has toward all creatures the function of *relation*—he is the living and effective synthesis, the angular and extant synthesis, the assuming and total synthesis of everything that exists, has existed and can exist, world and time without end.

If there is no total and effective synthesis possible in the human order, as several dream of it, it is because Christ alone is this synthesis, wholly hidden yet wholly living. To set forth this virtual view of Christian thought, and to illuminate it by considerations taken from our own time, to see what duty it proposes to the intelligence, what rule for action: such will be the object of this study.

The word "redemption" evokes first of all the work of ransom on the cross. It sums up the work of grace, at its highest point: the sacrifice of the Word incarnate in order to give life to the world, by effacing sin, by raising humanity to make it worthy of a divine existence. Formerly, faith was a common property: possessed by all, it could go to meet the intelligence in order to illuminate it, and social problems in order to solve them to boot. Nowadays, in Europe and in the unbelieving world, it is not faith which is called into question, but the foundation of faith: it is reason, justice, it is the idea of truth, it is the dignity of the person, it is nature itself. We are no longer citizens of a universe in which faith, given first, searches for the intelligence which will elucidate it. We are citizens of a world in which the intelligence, given first and believing itself totalitarian, attempts to organize man by itself and in which its sorely felt defeat is perhaps going to give it the idea of seeking a higher enlightenment.

And, consequently, it is less important to show that the redemption gives grace than to show that the redemption saves nature itself, and that the most solid possessions, which compose the natural order of the world, the acquisitions of which man is the proudest and the most sure, those which give to civilization its savor and its value, have *in fact* their source and their safeguard in the secret working of Christ: so that he is the hidden fountain and the invisible bond of the works which thought has conceived in forty centuries of historic development.

I will take several examples which I believe full of significance, in that they help to discern that which comes from man and that which comes from Christ in human works. And you will permit me to extend Christ to the dimensions of history, that is, when I speak of Christ, to consider, at the same time as the historic Christ, the anterior Christ prepared by the development of Israel, and the posterior Christ continued by the Church with the apostles and their successors. I choose, from among many others, two concepts to which the present time clings by its roots, and which are among us the subject of impassioned discussions: the concept of *love* and the concept of *history*. And I ask myself: what would they be outside of Christ? I have at my disposition, to solve this problem, the experience of great and noble civilizations in which the redemptive influence has not penetrated: antiquity at its most perfect degree of perfection, Greek antiquity, and the Hindu world with its mysteries and its sages.

Let us consider love. This tender, confiding and noble sentiment which binds forever a single man to a single woman has not been able to be completely ignored by humanity; but that which we call love implies an equality of man and woman, and outside the current of history directed toward the eternal Christ, woman remains a servant, sometimes privileged but always inferior in essence. The woman of antiquity is a piece of the domestic organism, the "matron" mother of citizens who satisfies the social function. Or else she is the mistress of the street corners, of the high places, who satisfies the erotic function. And even the sage Plato accepts this division of functions; for Plato, woman is but the occasion of the fire of Eros which ascends toward the Beautiful, toward the pure Idea: she is not the beloved, the unique, the *dilects* of the Song of Songs. It is necessary that Christ come, in order that the original unity of the first Adamic couple be re-established, and that woman, instead of being *dissociated* into "mother" and "mistress," be united to man and united to herself, in order that she become once more both she who engenders and she who is loved at one and the same time.

And everywhere that the synthesizing thought of Christ grows weaker, we see woman once more dissociate into two, we see reappear these two types of inferior woman, one of which is devoted to family generation without being loved in and for herself, the other of which is condemned to pleasure without being honored. But while honoring monogamous, indissoluble marriage and separating the new couple from father and mother in order to found a new community, the Christ elevates above marriage the virginity of consecration. He *restores* human love and *establishes* divine love, without opposing them to one another, but rather nourishing them on one another in the unity of the Church.

Let us consider the concept of history. Our century has discovered *history* and *time*. And, having discovered time and its movement, the thinkers have immediately opposed them to Christ, dissolving Jesus of Nazareth into Becoming and Evolution, like a point lost in the infinite of history, a necessary moment in its dialectic. They reduce Christ, the Master of time, to the single Nazarene who is an atom of history, whom they believe they have completely explained by the conditions of milieu, moment and chance. But who, then, has revealed the essence of the Idea of historic time, if not Christ? For before him and outside of him, history is reduced to a pure succession of events disposed upon a cyclic time, which reproduces itself eternally—in such a way that, for the ancient Greeks as for the Hindus, the "eternal return," dear to Nietzsche, brings back from period to period the same destinies. But such a conception, which would multiply infinitely the incarnation and the calvaries, which would oblige the saints to be reincarnated in all the cycles, is unacceptable to him who believes in Christ, come *once and for all*, in a singular *advent* which is also a definitive *event*, prepared by a long, progressive impetus, constituted by the development of the Church. As Cullmann has again recently shown (in the spirit of Newman, of Pascal, of St. Augustine and of St. Paul), Christ brings us *indirectly* the intellectual enlightenment which establishes history—that history which must be henceforth, after him, conceived not as a *wheel*, but as an *arrow*, having a beginning and an outcome, launched into being by the Creator, creating time by its passage. By that can be justified that living tradition, that creative conservation which one calls progress and which men of this time consider with reason as the ideal, although they are mistaken about the capacity of man loosed from Christ to promote moral progress. Thus, Christ has been in fact the revealer of history conceived as a directed, continuous, ascending current, formed of events which have posterity. Let us keep the thought that Christ is at the root of several of the great ideas in which our contemporaries "live, move and have their being." But, since they no longer believe in him who is the salt and the ferment of these ideas, the latter deteriorate in their hands, they dissociate. And, for example, the idea of love, dechristianized, leads them to worship the flesh, the heart, woman, passion, or even the torment of loving; the idea of history and of time, dechristianized, leads them to worship the movement of history. As if this state of flux were God himself or the necessary incarnation of God! As if history were not summoned to emerge into the eternal realm of God! As if history were at each moment the judge of history, and were not to be judged the day of the end of history, in the *parousia* of Christ the Judge!

One could make comparable analyses in regard to the majority of the great ideas by which we live, that of *person*, that of *community* for example, that of *humanism*, that of *existence*. I have only tried here to suggest researches, not forgetting my subject, which is that of synthesis. It is fitting here to underline the astonishing disparity which exists between the *right* and the *fact*. Indeed, by right, humanity could have found God the Creator on its own, and we know that, in fact, it has sometimes grazed him, but it has never found him in his purity outside of the current oriented toward Christ or sprung from him. By right, humanity could have conceived and realized a humane humanism, fully adapted to the dignity of man; in fact, outside of Christ, it has not conceived and above all not realized it. By right, humanity could have honored woman as a person; in fact, outside of Christ, it has not honored her as a person. By right, humanity could have pictured its own history, its progress, its individual or social duration; in fact, outside of Christ, it has not fully nor worthily pictured them. Everything takes place as if it had needed a gratuitous and transcendent assistance, not in order to find the order of grace and of undemandable gifts, but in order to find itself and to understand its own existence, its own nature. An experience stretched out over a duration of forty centuries and over all the peoples of this planet always makes this curious inconsequence stand out, between that which should have taken place and that which has taken place in reality. Man is incapable of being man without a divine assistance.

We come back to the guiding intuition which I suggested to you at the beginning. Christ is the bond of that which without him would be without consistency; he intervenes in order to give to the existence of the moral world its stability and its equilibrium, its purity and its savor, like a *cornerstone* which, strictly speaking, is not a part of the edifice (or, at least, which does not seem to be more than the other stones) and which is nevertheless the key of the arch and the principle of its immobile solidity. He is not exactly he who makes, but he who makes perfect and who (we shall soon see) remakes. He *by whom* everything was made, he in whom everything will be finally summed up and recapitulated. These expressions, so precise and so powerful, set forth the most profound thought of St. Paul, who was the first and the greatest of the thinkers whom Christianity has engendered. For, if one measures the power of thought by the diversity of the elements which it must both respect in their diversity and unite in synthesis, when was there ever, I ask you, so much diversity: the law of Moses, the religion of the patriarchs, the prophecies, Adam, the perenniality of the promises, the transcendent unity of God, the ancient order, divine fidelity —and on the other hand the faith in Jesus, the new ordinance, grace, the death of Jesus, his resurrection, the end of time, the renewal in the Christ, the new sacraments, evangelization, the continuation of history; all this among the interior perils of excessive conservatives or aberrant innovators, among the exterior perils of pagan gods, philosophies and The Empire. Well, St. Paul has no trouble uniting, for he has in him the principle of synthesis: it is the Christ who lives in him, in history and in the Church and in whom all existence will be summed up.

: : :

But here it is fitting, I think, to make an observation which is in the very spirit of St. Paul, although not formulated directly by him, and which I will present as follows. The synthesis effected by Christ is a synthesis respectful of each element which it assembles; it is a quiet and discreet synthesis which remains yet invisible except to the eyes of faith. The time will come in which this synthesis will appear in glory: then everything which is matter will die away, but everything which is form, nervure, architecture will remain; the mysterious moment will come in which the Son will appear and subordinate all things to himself, in order that God be "all in all." Beforehand, this ordination takes place in the depths, it remains wrapped in divine patience and humility.

Let us take up again certain of these points. I said that in this synthesis Christ respects each and every thing. A Greek philosopher asked himself the following question: "How does it come about that things form a unity and yet each is apart and by itself?" And, in the same spirit, Pascal observed that our art makes things enter into one another, while nature leaves them to themselves, *each one holding its own place*. It is fairly easy to obtain order by discipline and commandment, by making all one's followers alike, as one does in armies, but it is far more difficult to educate men by unifying them in one and the same spirit, while respecting their freedom and their individuality, making each one grow according to his own path—in short, giving them to themselves, each one, as God did by creating us in a manner so touching by its respect and discretion. Now, in this work of synthesis which Christ effects in the world and in history, what is so curious is his respect for the play of natures and freedoms. This had already fascinated St. Augustine when, thinking over his own history in order to see therein him who had called him in the midst of his dissoluteness, he noted that the hand of Christ, though sovereign, was the most gentle, to such a point that he did by himself that which grace was doing in him. And Newman remarked also that Christ, the Master of our destinies, was so respectful of our being that he disappeared in the present moment of his working, to manifest himself only in the recollection. But that which we observe in the mystery of our lives we find again on the scale of universal values. The presence of Christ, precisely because it is a total, intimate, enveloping presence, is a presence which does not make itself felt. That is why one notices through the course of history that the Christian influence gives being to being. It gives reason to reason and makes it more fully reasonable, just as it gives freedom to freedom, making it more fully free. In another domain, it helps states be wholly states in which Caesar looks after the affairs of Caesar; and, in keeping states from being temporal churches lording it over the soul, it gives to the state its true essence. Everywhere else, either in pagan antiquity, or in Islam, or in the Russia of the Soviets, the state tends to be also a church, and the totalitarian monarch makes use of minds as well as bodies. The influence of Christ helps nations to know themselves in their own mission, in their inalienable singularity; it gives them to themselves, as one saw for France in the marvelous moment of Joan of Arc. And one could go on and show this same kind of influence, preservative of essences and natures. It is with reason that one would reject the bond of Christ, if it alienated, as Feuerbach and Marx thought. But it does not *alienate*, it *constitutes*.

It constitutes, I say, without becoming visible outside; it harmonizes inwardly, without this harmony being necessarily visible. Père Lagrange, when he compared the Gospels and showed their profound convergence under the apparent contradictions, liked to cite the saying of Heraclitus: "The hidden harmony is better than the visible." There exist, as a matter of fact, two types of synthesis: the first type is that of visible synthesis, as, for example, in the architecture of the Parthenon, the poetry of Virgil or of Racine, or in classical art, which serves as a prime model. But there is also a second type of synthesis and harmony, that which reigns in a dissymmetrical landscape, in a tormented visage, in the uneven cadences of poetry, in the *Pensées* of Pascal, in *Hamlet* and in *Faust*, in the work of Claudel. Then, the bond which connects the parts of such works is found in the unity of bursting forth, in the affinity of each particle with the creative spirit, without there being any apparent order, but rather oppositions, quite strange passages, sudden ellipses. The most beautiful example of such an order in apparent disorder is perhaps that of the Roman Mass: it is composed of fairly disparate prayers and rites, some long, some concise; here ellipses, there repetitions. No apparent harmony, but what a rapid and sublime symphony! And where is the bond of all its elements found if not in the presence of the immolated and glorious Christ? This is a symbol of the action of Christ in the universe of minds and of works. The order which he establishes by his synthetic action is an intimate, profound order, a silent, discreet, unfathomable order and, if I dare say it, a humble order which does not impose itself as if it came from an exterior force, but which proposes itself from within. This order comes from the fact that each nature, being sound like a well cut and precisely placed stone, plays its role in the total edifice. In *The Tidings Brought to Mary,* Claudel speaks to us of that cathedral called *Justice,* because everything there is very correctly and precisely articulated. It is the image of the spiritual community, of that mystic Jerusalem made of living rocks of which Christ is the foundation, the summit and the cement—the Christ who, because he is everywhere, is noticeable nowhere.

And perhaps one could say here that if Christ, although he is the synthesis, did not want to be visible, it is because every synthetic bond is precisely an inexpressible bond, being order, relation and proportion; and it is also because he wanted to reduce himself to nothing, although he is everything, and taste that divine delight, being everything, of being taken for nothing. The host which the ostensory offers us is the symbol of this mystery of a substantial bond, omnipresent and yet hidden from regards, reduced to nothing in the very moment that it vivifies.

If it is true first of all that the operation of Christ is an operation of assembling in unity and in a superior and profound unity, may that counsel seeking in everything the highest syntheses! The operation of genius consists in finding analogies and resemblances among the domains which are seemingly the most distant. The genius of the poet is in the choice of those exquisite, new and surprising metaphors which help to discern the unifying operation of the Creator among the separate sections of nature. The genius of the savant is in the seizure of those simple and universal relations which associate the infinitely large and the infinitely small under one and the same law. The genius of the statesman or the strategist is in the application of several very simple principles in ever varied executions, to such a point that Napoleon said that he had learned nothing since his first battle. The genius of the artist and of the philosopher is to draw from their spirit an infinitely simple intuition which resembles them and which resembles everything, thus relating their singular soul to the universal architecture of forms. In all things, genius is to surmount. And I also believe that, on the order of discussion between men of good will, in everything which is struggle, controversy, even conflict, genius is to apply that rule of Lacordaire: "I do not try so much to prove my adversary guilty of error as to unite myself to him in a higher truth."

Another consequence: another resemblance of our labor

with the redemptive work. If it is true that the synthetic operation of Christ is respectful of essences and even disappears under unconcerned forms, then the Christian, in our times at least, does not have to impose Christ in an extrinsic, authoritarian way, too soon triumphant. He must not superadd Christ, as one adds a helmet to a head. Still less must he destroy in the name of Christ that which has been done outside of Christ and which is often good. Those who have acted thus in western history have been carried away by an intemperate zeal; and we observe that they have retarded the work of redemption by falsifying the image of Christ, that is, by substituting for Christ, unifier and repairer, a Christ who seemed to be a tyrant and alienator. Let us consider once more the work of Jesus in his era and in his milieu. What do we see? He accepted that which was ordained by his times: but he gave ferments in order to regenerate it without unsettling it. He left things as they were, even in the religion of Israel and in the Roman empire, but he placed himself in the midst of everything, just as, as a child, he placed himself in the center of the circle of doctors. And, under the influence of this presence, the religion of Moses was sublimed. The religion of Rome was annihilated.

Likewise, it is important to the intellectual to be present everywhere as a ferment to vivify that which is done without him and outside of him, to sort it, to remove from it the element of corruption or of excessiveness, to give it thus a pure fecundity. It has often come about, in the course of history, that the inventive dynamism has not been given to the children of Christ: it is not always they who have renewed the visage of the human sciences. But to Christians has been given an assimilating ferment which has kept this inventive dynamism from dissipating.

I would now like to open other perspectives which will make us enter into the intimity of the redemption. For, up to now, we have stayed as at the surface, for we had not spoken of sin, to which the redemption is in fact principally directed.

Up to now, moreover, we have been able to amble along with those who did not accept the totality of our faith, with "the philosophers and the savants," as Pascal said, with those who do not recognize "the God of Abraham, of Isaac and of Jacob." It is necessary now to enter upon new regions, which are nevertheless not unknown to men, but which they are not willing to regard carefully, nor to call by their name. Each year, for more than thirty years now, I have brooded over some great philosopher, whose doctrine I try to expose, to examine thoroughly—with the constant preoccupation of seeking by what this doctrine enlightens me about myself, or about human nature. Now, in reading the philosophers not directly touched by the ray of Christ—for example, the Greeks, the Alexandrians, the Stoics, the disciples of Spinoza and of Hegel, and nowadays Husserl or the Marxist philosophers—I am struck by seeing how little place the refractory element of human existence holds in their thought—the element which one can call failure, grief, sin, death, helplessness, humiliation, temporal dissipation. To be sure, these philosophers do not deny these undeniable experiences; but they turn their regard away from them; or rather, they accord them but an accidental value: they are flaws, accidents, "failures," provisional or apparent elements which derive from the maladjustment of the thinking species to the cosmos, from the awkwardness of man, from the state of infancy in which hygiene, industry find themselves, or else again from the injustice of the tyrant or of the propertied class. All that, as one says, "is called upon to disappear." There will be a day on the earth when there will no longer be any grief. But this view, which was that of the great minds of the nineteenth century—of Comte, for example, of Spencer, of Renan, of Marx—and which is still presupposed in all political discourses by an effect of retentivity, could nowadays no longer be maintained with sincerity by those who think. Experience protests after so many "last wars," that is, so many wars, each one of which was conceived of as the last of the wars. In this respect, the development of the thought of that great mind, Henri Bergson, is full of meaning. Toward 1906, at the age of "the sweetness of living," when Bergson wrote *Creative Evolution,* he affirmed that the vital impetus present in humanity was capable of progressing and of regenerating itself by itself, that a superman was perhaps going to appear, and that, at least, progressing humanity was capable of clearing all obstacles, "perhaps even death." When one is acquainted with the intimate and secret life of Bergson, one knows that these expressions, purposely vague, masked for him an implicit adherence to Christianity and that the superman was to be understood in the sense of St. Paul and not in the sense of Nietzsche. Twenty-five years later, in 1933, when Bergson wrote *The Two Sources of Morality and Religion,* he had stated these views precisely: he clearly admitted that man, if he were left to himself, if he did not participate in that mystical superhumanity of the prophets, of Christ and of the saints, could but close up upon or degrade himself. In his last conversations, collected by Père Sertillanges and Jacques Chevalier, he said that the Gospel had become his true spiritual fatherland, "and nothing of what Christ there says of himself either astonishes or disappoints me." But, previously, in a letter to Daniel Halévy in regard to the death of Péguy, speaking of his disciple with whom he seemed to identify himself, he said that Péguy had drawn ever nearer to "him who took upon himself the sins and distresses of humankind." Thus Bergson recognized in the substance of man an indomitable element: as Pascal put it, it was necessary, all things considered, to "stretch out one's arm to the liberator." Heidegger and his existentialist disciples have followed the same path, although they have stopped at the half-way point and have from then on divinized anxiety. For it is a law of human weakness that it raises to the absolute that which it has not the force to surpass.

But if it is true that a certain dose of downfall and of grief, of sin and of compensating suffering enters into the composition of the human world—for this world to be offered by the Word-made-man, it does not suffice that it be pacified, unified, raised and sublimed—it is necessary in addition and above all that it be repaired, restored, rebuilt and, as we put it, *redeemed*. It does not suffice that it be concentrated, in full bloom and complete—it must also be bandaged, cicatrized and healed. Humanity, to take comparisons from the Gospel, is not comparable to a traveler who must be put on the track, guided and preceded, but to a traveler fallen into the ditch, robbed and injured, in despair; it is not comparable to a sheep to be led to pasturage, but to a lamb which has lost its way far from any path and become entangled in the brambles. It is not like a son whom one would raise as one's heir, but like a prodigal son whom one would have to re-educate in order to restore him into the house of his father.

This is a constant and integral aspect of the human condition. There is nothing human which can satisfy itself, that does not have the tendency to relapse, to become corrupt. And the enemy of man is not his adversary, it is he himself in the ill-founded love which he has for himself.

We perceive this law of existence in the big as in the small. Societies become corrupt; the means of doing good become means of doing evil; brothers murder one another; sons rebel; the skills of man turn against man; the old law of the tower of Babel has its present-day application in the atomic affair. That which appears on the universal scale is found again more strikingly for us on the singular scale: the projects of youth run aground, the visage of man happy to go ahead makes room for the visage of the man of sorrows; man sins and torments himself; and, before he has been able to reach fruition, death intervenes to interrupt. As man advances on the line of time which he sees growing shorter, as humanity advances also on this same line and envisages (thus, at the present moment) its last hour as a possible eventuality, then there comes to the mind of singular man and of universal man the impression that life is coming to an end without anything being attained, that we want that which we do not do, that we do that which we do not want.

It is here that the redemption, taken in its fullest sense, finds its most profound significance. I am among those who think, with St. Bonaventure and Duns Scotus, that Christ would have become incarnate even if we had not sinned, in order to raise humanity in him to the highest degree of excellence, of simplicity and of glory. But since in fact man was hardly able not to sin as time went on, the incarnation, without changing its nature or its original aim, became redemptive, as the sun at its setting, because it leans toward the earth to unite with it intimately, is tinged with tears of light and appears under the sign of blood. At this moment the sun remains still the source of light, but of light more tender and more sacrificed. This is the thought, I believe, of St. Paul, in the opening hymn of Ephesians, for example. But let us consider that which results from this view in relation to the synthetic power which we are endeavoring to point out in the action of the Word incarnate, of the historic and yet eternal Christ.

If Christ is the great inner unifier of everything in time

which is destined for eternity, if he is the maker of peace, the pacifier, the architect of passageways and bridges, the *pontifex*, the high priest, it was conceivable—as the Epistle to the Hebrews, developing the thought of St. Paul, suggests—that he "learned obedience by these sufferings" (Heb 5:8) which he had assumed in obedience to his Father; and that this obedience was total, that is to say, that he loved unto death and "the death of the cross," which completed, consummated, linked together, illuminated everything which went before it. Thus Jesus synthesized everything: *faciebat utraque unum*, by the blood of the cross. Let us say here: by the synthetic operation of suffering accepted in love, in the spirit of reparation. Let us reflect upon the value of suffering considered as a factor of peace, of restoration, of unity regained.

If sin is divisive and dissociative, suffering is essentially unifying, structure-giving, restoring, revivifyng and synthetic. The suffering of love is synthesis itself. In it, the physical pain assumed by a good being unites him to this good, the divine will, and thereby dissolves the moral evil. In it, passivity becomes activity of assent. Through it, the contradictory terms are wedded: thus the fury of the executioner and the mildness of the martyr. And the doers of evil are saved by their victim. The death of Stephen saves the executioners and engenders Paul to the Church . . . Suffering assumed, without masochism or moroseness, is living dialectic. It unites the earth and the heaven. And the *cross*, with its two directions, vertical and horizontal, traced on the dimensions of a human body stretched out and raised, is the symbol of this dialectic which unites that which is the lowest with that which is the highest, and which repairs any fall and even any mediocrity.

You then perceive in a new light this synthetic aspect of the redemption, so favorable for intellectual meditation. Perhaps it has not yet been made prominent enough by thought. One has often left the bleeding visage of the Man of Sorrows to piety, to love, to restoring adoration, without sufficiently considering the calm, profound and unifying operation of suffering. If we reread the prayer of oblation of the Lord in chapter 17 of John, we would see how much it is a clarifying (*Clarifica Filium tuum*) source of total and unifying joy, making of the beings given to Christ a unity comparable to the triune unity. And, if the Eucharist is a memorial of the passion and an oblation continued in fact, it is at the same time and for that very reason bread of life and bond of unity. Who has grasped better than St. Thomas this hidden bond of the passion to the truth of structures, of the Eucharist to the intimate life of the intelligence?

There is thus a relationship between the work of redemption and the work of intelligence. And this analogy manifests itself also in the very function of intellectual work, which cannot be accomplished unaccompanied by suffering. In all work of the mind, above all in that work in which the mind searches for some new relationships, some affinity as yet unknown of being or of language, some new synthesis, it is necessary, as Pascal said, to "offer oneself, by humiliations to inspirations, which alone have the true and salutary effect." The former are not lacking, since our intelligence incarnate exerts itself in an intractable body, in a social milieu often refractory. Nothing is ever easy. And, if ever a thing appeared easy, we would have to say to ourselves that it deceives us; it would be necessary to do it in a difficult way. We also know well that there are deserts of patience; that "one does the planting, and another the reaping" (Jn 4:37); that the truth is not beloved of men, and that one must expect their indifference, if not their scorn; finally, that the greatest grief is not that which others cause you, but that which oneself causes to onself by one's own helplessness.

This aspect of struggle and of grief, inherent in the human substance and which binds us to Christ incarnate, is perhaps more real in our age than in any other. Not, to be sure, that sufferings have been lacking in each generation; but because man, in developing his intelligence and his skill, has developed also his faculty of feeling and of suffering. On the other hand, barriers having fallen between peoples and telecommunications having given the human race a nervous system, men are tending to become bound together. Humanity resembles a single, magnified body. Yes, the time is coming when humanity taken as a whole is going to resemble man. Like man, whose form we feel in each one of us, humanity in its great body is going to feel divided against itself, very strong and very weak, king and slave, capable at every moment of rising above itself or of destroying itself, like an adolescent infatuated with the infinite, fingering a revolver in his pocket. I sometimes say: "Perhaps the moment of the *passion* of humanity is beginning?" Every man knows his own passion. Nations, in order to grow or to come into existence, have also known their passion and know it still, like Germany. But perhaps the time will come when humanity, taken as a whole, is going to suffer no longer separately, each of its members suffering apart and differently, but this time all humanity together and of the same evil. Then it will assume the visage of the Man of Sorrows, he of whom Pilate said: *Behold the man.*

Let this not trouble those who declare that humanity has been summed up in Christ and that it has already undergone in its head a passion of redemption, pledge of glory. Let it help to discern the work of the redemption in a less conventional way.

Instead of bemoaning ourselves, like those who have no hope, let us give thanks to God to have been born in this century and to live at the pivot of this age of universal metamorphosis in this moment in which everything seems compromised, but in which everything is more living, more conscient, more bound together, more unified than in any time lived by the ancient, and yet so young human race—in which, consequently, the synthetic work of Christ has become more sensible to the heart and more pressing.

We are in a time of Pentecost, speaking diverse languages, united in one and the same Spirit. In this time of a great council, we raise our intelligences toward Christ; we earnestly entreat him that he obtain from the Father that the synthesis of humanity, perhaps its last unification, not come about by a *total war* but by a *total synthesis.* We ask him to manifest himself to this generation as being himself the definitive bond, the "cornerstone," as the first Pope said on the first day of the Church. Meanwhile, we repeat to ourselves the maxim of St. Paul to the Philippians: that whatever is true, that whatever is just, that whatever is honorable, that whatever is lovable and pure be the food of our thought (Phil 4:8). We must cooperate in everything good which is done in the world, for we possess—without being worthy of it—the ferment without which the bread of men would be without savor. We bear, we Christians, in our heavy mediocrity, the sole essential element which is lacking to the others in order to unite them.

3 THE THIRD WORLD AND ECUMENISM

The number three has always had a profound significance, because the third term announces the synthesis and the plenitude. And one could more modestly propose this law, which is going to dominate my whole subject: *every time that a third term intervenes, the relations of the two other terms are modified,* for better or for worse. The type of this nuclear modification is the appearance of the first child into the conjugal mystery. More generally, it is the presence of the guest, of the visitor, of the beggar, of the poor. Tertullian called the Christians the third world, *tertium genus humanum,* and it is a fact that the arising of this third, Christian term has substantially modified the relations of the two worlds, Gentile and Jewish, as St. Paul had had an inkling of it in Romans. Nowadays we see between the West and the East, between the world called capitalist and the world called communist, between the Catholic world and the non-Catholic world, a Third World looming up. And the question which I am going to ask myself—simple in its wording, very complex in its solution—you can guess that it is the following: *To what extent are the appearance of this third world and the duty of evangelization which this appearance awakens in the Christian confessions going to transform ecumenical relations?* You can gauge the urgency, the depth, the scope and also the great delicateness of this problem in which the highest questions of mission, of faith, of conscience are engaged in a very new way.

❨ 1

I will start from an undeniable fact, which is the obstacle presented by our divisions. As it is, these divisions often paralyze the missionary effort among the nonbelievers of our world. But how much more so in a new country without history! A Protestant missionary has said: "It is a veritable tragedy not to be able to present oneself as one single church when we work in the mission field." The tragic comes from the fact that one bears, by the spectacle of the discord about the faith, a *counter-proof* of the truth of the faith, of the force of love. One undoes what one is doing at the very moment. One scandalized instead of evangelizing.

This tragic problem has already had a happy effect in Christian consciences. It has awakened the ecumenical sense. The missionary responsibility has had the effect of exciting the ecumenical vocation. It is because we, both Protestants and Catholics, have awakened to our apostolic duty toward this third, unbelieving or atheistic world, which is tending to become organized and which could conquer the entire earth, that we have felt the duty of reducing our differences and of taking more seriously the prayer of our unique Christ and Lord for the unity of his Church.

But this duty is hard to fulfill! What a lot of unsatisfying solutions! I see one right away which is very tempting for the mind and which would nonetheless be worse than the evil. It consists in formulating a faith which would realize the union and the intercommunion of Christians, either by a sub-Christianity or by a super-Christianity. I call sub-Christianity that agreement on the least common denominator of our confessions: for example, on a vague evangelism, such as Rousseau professes in the *Vicaire savoyard*. I call super-Christianity that agreement on a dialectical synthesis of Catholicism and Protestantism which would reconcile them by pushing each to its limit, as Leibniz seems to have conceived it. The greatness, the force, the religious authenticity of current ecumenism is to reject equally these two false unities. To be sure, our divisions can create a scandal, but they testify to an absolute attachment to what I will call the virginity of divine truth. In the domain of essence, we do not admit of concession, nor of compromise. Our divisions have political, psychic, social causes: but the reason which maintains them in the most pure consciences is the obligation of following the will of Jesus Christ such as we perceive it and of preferring a torn but authentic robe to a robe without rent, but which would be obtained by artifice.

The Third World will in the beginning find it quite difficult to understand this. But is this to say that, in order to preserve the chastity of our adherence, we should present ourselves before the Third World as adversaries, separated from one another? I here touch upon a question extremely delicate in theory as in practice. I leave out all the detail and the particular, in order to indicate the axis of the solution which I envisage.

It seems to me highly desirable that both Protestants and Catholics, instead of envisaging and presenting our faith as a monolithic bloc without levels, agree to discern within it *distinct levels of adhesion and generality*. In the faith which we preach to the world, there exist a structure and strata of different amplitude. For example, there is first of all the fundamental base of the truths common and natural to man, which make possible a first dialogue with any man come into this world. Then there is the level, less broad of base, of the belief in Christ, Son of God, Savior: the essential level, the level of Christian witness! Then there is the level of the faith in the Church, as she assures the presence of the Gospel through space and time. This is the level where our differences are situated. Who does not feel that on the antecedent planes we can see our efforts converge, under one essential condition which I want to define: it is that at whatever level we have arrived, we do not decide that that level is a closed level, covered with a roof, spiked with thorns, implying a final, exclusive term. If the level of human nature closes itself and refuses God, it is naturalism, secularism, sometimes atheism. If the level of God closes itself, it is the anti-trinitarian monotheism of Islam. If the level of the Gospel closes itself, it is "evangelism" in the negative and diminished sense of the word.

I know too well, from having read the accounts of the oppositions of Protestants and Catholics in mission country, that grave difficulties arise at the ecclesial, sacramental level. Protestants and Catholics cannot here be in communion, and although the theologians and exegetes diminish the differences and delimit a common platform broader than yesterday (in what concerns the notion even of the Church, of ecclesiastical tradition, of sacramental life), there still remain abysms to fill in. There is our grief.

But here is what I for my part would ask of the missionaries. No indiscreet, injurious and violent proselytism; few discussions; an effort to set forth one's faith in a positive, reasoned manner, based on Scripture and tradition without attacks on the other; above all an exacting exercise of love of the other in Christ in order to *understand* his different faith, in order to admit that crucifying but true paradox according to which the conviction that each one has of being in the unique Church of Christ has the same inner principle: the attachment to this same Lord equally adored and whom each one is ready to follow, if he manifests to him more clearly his holy will in order to lead us there where we were not willing to go. This attitude which reconciles on a high plane or, if I dare say, on Calvary, the truth and the respect of the other consciences, demands a supreme tension: but the ecumenical spirit is not a spirit of facility. It has its nights.

It remains that a witness can be borne. As a young pastor said to an ecumenical assembly:

"At bottom, we all bear witness for one and the same Lord. In England, for example, when an Anglican and a

Baptist meet in a factory, their respective points of view on the episcopacy are relegated to the middle distance, while their witness rendered to one and the same Christ remains in the foreground. In affirming this, we do not take our doctrinal differences lightly. . . . But we simply mean that there is a unity in witness, of which many among us have had the experience in the difficult years of the war.

"While waiting for the unity desired by Christ to be realized integrally, is it not possible to plane down a little, for unbelievers, the stumbling block: by making them feel the core of profound unity which exists among all Christians, beyond the divisions?

"It cannot be a question of sinning against one's inner conviction by an intercommunion which did not correspond to a sufficient sharing of the same faith. But, without artificially masking the separations, it is possible to make manifest the bonds: bonds of faith and bonds of charity supported by both Protestants and Catholics. The more one emphasizes the common beliefs, the more one succeeds in understanding and approaching one another by the heart, and the more one can then help one another mutually in order to give a common spring (instead of paralyzing one another)."

I believe that if one agreed to consider what I have called the structure of belief, several difficulties would be alleviated. And, while assuring the integrity of one's faith, one would have the joy of being in communion with broader and broader expanses of consciences which, not participating in our total faith, share nonetheless certain zones of adhesion.

❡ 2

We have just seen, under a first aspect, how the appearance of this third term of the Third World could be for separated Christians the occasion to diminish certain of their divergences, giving their faith more solidity and intelligence, envisaging it in relief and in depth. One would thus renounce the polemical confrontment of past centuries in order to achieve a common, parallel and ecumenical front, yet without seeking the denominator of compromise of which I said that it would be a mutual betrayal.

But there is more. And I would like to analyze with more precision, and discover in a way which I believe more intimate, the purifying fecundity of this third term.

In order to make myself understood, I introduce an axiom which is dear to me and which I formulate as follows: when two consciences, separated for reasons which they judge considerable, want to come together again, the sacrificial effort cannot be one-sided. The blood, although in a different way, must be shed by both the transpierced hearts. Catholics, I know, have often forgotten this axiom. John XXIII did not forget it—he who for five years did not cease saying that the Church, in order to pave the way for unity, must first of all make an immense effort of renewal, of rejuvenation, of revitalization upon herself. Now, the two worlds—Catholic and non-Catholic, or West-East—how do they appear in the eye of the Third World?

They appear like a single world of western, technocratic, imperial and propertied Christianity, one could almost say:

as a Christianity provided for and materialized, giving to the word "matter" the sense of wealth, of concept, of technique, of art, of splendor and of *having*, the sense in which Marcel opposes *having* and *being*. And the Third World is troubled. It sees, it has an inkling that the Christian missionary brings it an essence, an enlightenment, a divine energy—new and unmerited—which it lacks for perfecting and subliming itself, so that "that which in it is mortal be assumed by life." But this *treasure*, the Third World sees it in *vessels* which are not fragile but artificial, and according to appearances, deceptive, since the possessive mentality (be it, moreover, of a capitalist or communist kind), comes to smother, obscure, corrupt the message of Christ Jesus.

The sense of the spiritual life (as superior to comfort and to all matter), daily confidence, kindness, the spirit of contemplation, the feeling of an immediate divine presence at the heart of the cosmos, the sense of being rooted in the tradition of one's ancestors, respect for the sacredness of the dead, constant communion with the world of spirits and divine messengers, love of the unanimous life of the community, respect for the guest and the voyager . . . , how many "values," as they are called, the Third World knows and practices better than civilized men, superior and proud of their abstraction, of their individualism, of their self-assurance, of their technique and of their wealth! And, to sum everything up, this underdeveloped and dispossessed world, whose standard of living is often so low in comparison with ours, could teach us what we take care not to ask of it: a spirit of divestment, a certain renunciation of anticipation in the sense in which it is a possession; in a word, the poverty of the first Beatitude. Rich, we bring them the Gospel of the beatitudes, and they could reply: "That which you do not do, that is what you preach to us."

: : :

The Third World has the tendency to confuse the bourgeoise West with Christianity. It is important for Christians, by their words and by their behavior, to work to dissipate this confusion. The West is the meeting place of extremes: the purest spiritualism, linked to Christianity, and dogmatic and practical materialism.

On the one hand, it is necessary to disengage, in the western heritage, the spiritualistic and Christian side, always fecund as soon as it is found again without compromise—while separating out the materialistic side. On the other hand, it is necessary to show that this spiritualistic West is but one of the possible incarnations of Christianity; that the Christian incarnation must inform other cultures by taking on new aspects, by respecting and making fruitful that which is best in these other cultures. And for that, in a large measure, Christianity must shed the old garments of mentalities already traversed, as the insect sheds its chrysalis.

Not only is this work necessary in order to convert the peoples of the Third World without violating them or making them anemic by ruining their natural and legitimate riches; but it is perhaps indispensable in order to regenerate western Christianity itself, by stripping it of that which is outdated in the mentalities which it takes on and by purifying it in this way. Not that it has to renounce all the values of its own tradition: it is of its terrestrial nature that it has constantly to develop what is alive in this tradition. But it is necessary to prune the dead branches which ruin the vitality of the tree and which smother the green boughs.

: : :

New spiritualities must spring up in our era. Spiritualities of the Third World. Spiritualities also of the West, awakened to the religious sense. And there again, "the final cause, the soul of the movement," will be "in the feeling of a disparity between the eternal Gospel and the Church" of our time. As a Carmelite Father told me: "A spirituality is the exigency of a deficiency." If we retain this definition, it will enlighten us.

The ecumenical consciousness is the consciousness of a deficiency in unity. Yes, it is a ferment which these days can raise the Christian dough, and through it, the whole human dough.

Let us say here that it will be necessary to take care not to present, either to the West or to the Third World, spiritualities at a discount, in which one would separate out the difficult and the heroic under the pretext of "accommodating them to modern life." As Bergson said, the enormous growth of our material powers demands a "*supplement* of soul." There is need of spiritualities which, under a new form, demand just as much and still more inner deepening and well-thought-out asceticism than the most lofty spiritualities of the Middle Ages. In the age in which sports demand preparations so much more extended than the Olympiads of St. Paul, in which scientific research requires an unprecedented intellectual asceticism, in which war becomes "total"—the inner life could not be content with elementary good intentions and with our slight desires of "*homo loquax.*" The enormous technical refinements, which our material improvements and the "forcing" of our inventive intelligence impose upon us, demand a culture proportionally just as elaborated from the point of view of the life of the soul. This for the West. As for the "Third World," it has a spirituality in certain respects superior to ours, to the extent that it has not been mechanized by our materialistic civilization. It is necessary not to present it a Christianity which would seem to it contemptible.

(In this respect, the nomination by John XXIII of so many cardinals sprung from *religious* orders has a certain symbolic aspect.)

: : :

Thus, from the ecumenical point of view, the realization of the obstacle of our divisions for the mission can help us to confront with more courage the problem of obedience to Christ—which is, for both Protestants and Catholics, the substance of the problem. The *mission* of Christ and the *union* of Christ are reciprocal imperatives. It is necessary to be united in Christ in order for the mission to the Third World to be efficacious, authentic and divine. And, in return, the sacrifices, the anxious appeals of the missionaries oblige us to desire the unity of Christians. *Henceforth the two problems are linked: the truly universal evangelical mission and the unity of the Church, truly one.* We do not yet see the *how* of this relationship. We contemplate the exigency of it in faith.

And for that the Third World helps us. I will readily say that it brings us, by the stripping off of our veneers, a means of *purity*. And that we bring to it, by the benediction of Christ, a means of *plenitude*. Now, the ecumenical Church for which we work is the painful union of *purity* and *plenitude*, those two dimensions of the cross which intersect at the heart.

And, just as the third man, there on the road of Emmaus —glorious, dispossessed, an unknown voyager—changed the relation of the two men who listened to the Word and the call until the evening's breaking of the bread, so is it permitted to hope that the meeting with the Third World will hasten the hour of union of Christians.

PART TWO

HISTORY OF THE THOUGHT

1 ACTUALITY OF LEIBNIZ

1
The Union of Christians

The problems posed by the division of Christians are not new. They have been within the scope of thinkers of the first rank; they were discussed many times when the first effects of the Reformation were making themselves felt. They have occupied philosophical and theological minds. In particular, they retained the attention of the broadest and most profound thinker of Europe of the seventeenth century: Leibniz. It can even be said that it was the concern for working for the unity of Christians which was the first spring of Leibniz's thought.

It is in view of a grand design, which is to diminish the oppositions of Christians, with an eye to reuniting them, that he becomes aware of his philosophical vocation. And his perspicacious genius discerns already the dogmas which provide the most difficulty, the principal one of which is the Catholic doctrine on the Eucharist. It is the meditation on "transubstantiation" which introduces him to that constant reflection on *substance* which will be the center and the mainspring of his metaphysics. Likewise, the meditation on "predestination," a subject of controversy, will have an influence on his philosophy of the monad and will color it until the end. Here we are before an ecumenical intellect, which perceives the analogical link of all problems and their relation with the extremely difficult problem of the unity of Christians after the Reformation.

At the beginning of the *Theodicy* Leibniz speaks of two insoluble problems: one for the geometrician, which is that of infinity, the other for the common man, which is that of predestination. There exists a third in the religious sphere, which is that of ecumenism: for no mediation seems to be able to ever unite the two forms of Christian aspiration, Protestantism and Catholicism. Leibniz dreams of being, here again, by the invention of a new method of integration to the infinite, that conciliator.

The spirit in which Leibniz works at ecumenism is magnanimous. He applied to the utmost his great practical rule, which is to act always for the best, but to believe that the failure of this action with an eye to the best is better still: for it substitutes for the hasty and personal love of the good the assent to the slowness of the hidden designs of God, who has need of our crosses, of our disappointments, of our failures, even of our faults (*o felix culpa!*) in order to compose secretly what Leibniz called *the optimum* and which will one day be revealed to us.

Leibniz wrote, for example, to Mme de Brinon concerning the unionist labor: "I have two maxims: one, to put everything to work to contribute to some good, the other, to be perfectly content when I do not succeed, being persuaded that in this case, it is for the best, that God doesn't will it at the present time. I do my part as long as there is hope, and I am content with his, when there is no longer any hope" (May 15, 1699).[1]

Leibniz had realized that the reunion of the churches was to be prepared discretely by mediations, unofficial initiatives, friendships between diplomats and mystics.

Often the way of the Spirit progressed along the paths of individual friendship. Thus Christophe de Rojas Spinola, the confessor of the Empress after the death of Philip IV, then Bishop of Tina in Croatia, then of Neustadt, had established a friendship with one of the most moderate among the Lutheran theologians, Gérard Valther Van der Muelen, Abbé of Lokkum, the famous Molanus. Spinola and Molanus drew up together a *Regula circa christianorum omnium ecclesiasticam Unionem*. After the death of Spinola in 1695, Bossuet had correspondence with Molanus, before knowing Leibniz.

And it must also be remembered that women have never been absent, in the background, from these ecumenical

[1] In the same spirit, Abbé Couturier wrote to Pastor Schutz: "Man proposes and God disposes . . . Our meeting was not in the plan of God. For you and for us there is but one possible attitude: Glory to God! That his will be done!—A failure? What grace! What proof! There is a divine mystery which escapes us and which we must adore in love. Our progress with unity has just taken a great stride! God has permitted us a failure!!! He is thus preparing great things. It is for us to let ourselves be purified, to let ourselves be impoverished of our desires, of our views, of our own will. We must enter into a great, divine mystery, that of suffering, a mystery in which future reconciliations are slowly forged." (*Ecclesia* 154, January 1962, 178).

friendships. Between Bossuet and Leibniz one sees appear the princess Louise-Hollandine, daughter of Frederick V, King of Bohemia, as well as Mme de Brinon.

Leibniz is ecumenical in the full sense of the word, more than any other Christian of his time; all his efforts are directed to repairing the scission of Christianity. He does not belong to the Roman Church; yet, we have the impression that by a supreme act of intelligence, he does not cease taking the point of view of that Church. That already distinguishes him from Protestantism and relates him to that unsubmissive fidelity which was that of the Jansenists and modernists, before and even after the condemnations of the Roman see. Unlike the Protestant who has left the Church in order to reproduce her outside in her purity, the modernist is insistent on remaining in the body of the Church in order to work for her reform. Pascal, as a Jansenist, shared in this state of mind. Not for an instant did he think of leaving the Church: he saw in Jansenism neither a heresy nor a sect, but the party in which, by a privilege of the Spirit, the authentic meaning of tradition was preserved.

Leibniz turned his attention to the *general cases* posed to him by the separated members of humanity, eager to be united. In this domain of union between the parties his work was analogous to that of the casuist. The casuist attempts to mark out inside a precept the minimum absolutely obligatory; this circle once traced, he arranges the periphery: an indefinite domain of concessions, mediations, conveniences. In like manner Leibniz determined the strictly indispensable which the possessory party could demand. One can disengage from his work the elements of an "ecumenical casuistry."

Leibniz indicated certain points where the Catholic Church could manifest a spirit of concession: communion under both species, the extension of special Masses, the justification of the sinner, the marriage of ecclesiastics, the validity of ordinations which would be performed among Protestants, divine worship in the vernacular, the episcopal rights of Protestant priests. He thought that the pope could grant these things, taken in a reasonable way, without offending the principles of the Roman Catholic Church.[2]

One of his principles consisted in the distinction between what is *best* and what is *necessary*. Leibniz remarked that that which is best is not always absolutely necessary, and he gave as an example the institution of monogamy, absent from the ancient law. It is remarkable to see how Leibniz had foreseen the modes of integration of the Protestants in the transitional period, so necessary to foresee in all great changes.

Thus, according to Leibniz, the Protestants would be able to keep their own disciplinary practices: communion under both species, and even marriage of ministers. One will distinguish between the necessary "beliefs" and the unnecessary "opinions." And the Protestants will remain in the Church as a religious order having special rites or else like the Eastern Catholic communities. Leibniz, whose mind had the genius of transitions, offered very concrete

[2] Des Méthodes de réunion (*Oeuvres*, ed. Foucher de Careil, II, 17).

suggestions, which certain others were to take up later without suspecting that he had put them forward. For example, it is noteworthy that Leibniz had seen that the study of the Anglican ritual could be a principle of union between the Catholics and the Protestants.

Leibniz sought an equivalent of the infallibility of the Church which could be accepted by the reformed. He found it:

The Church, he said, could be mistaken, but not in such a way that she damn us or incur damnation herself. A Catholic was thus never obliged to leave the Church in order to find salvation, no more than a Protestant could be obliged to enter it in order to find salvation; each was to remain in his place. Thus the Church was not strictly *infallible*, but she was *undamnable*.

This great mind, so apt at taking the other's point of view, did not realize that this middle term (like many of his mediations) was completely on the Protestant side and that it could thus not serve as a passage: the arch of the bridge remained on a single bank.

Leibniz would like more conformity to tradition in practices, more breadth in the relations with the Catholic Church. And, at the same time, he proposes reforming Catholicism by securing the rational connection of its doctrines, their consonance with primitive times, by furnishing justification of the dogmas apparently the most inadmissible to modern men (like the resurrection and transubstantiation), by showing the appropriateness of practices in appearance corrupt (like the worship of the saints or private masses), finally by offering plans of reform for the religious orders and giving directives concerning the mission of the Church in the world. Doing this, he pleases (so he believes, at least) both parties. Besides diminishing by infinitely small quantities several misunderstandings about details, he prepares to the limit union which will ask neither of the opposing parties to abjure its faith. Thus one progresses toward the ideal Church, where the present Churches find themselves "more noble than in themselves." And, the reunion once accomplished, the differences which would still remain by the weight of the past and its indistinct perception would tend to disappear, as do the differences in the calculation of the infinite.

"You are right," Leibniz wrote to Mme de Brinon, "to say that, in the way in which we are going about it, it seems that the Catholics would all become also Protestant and that the Protestants would become Catholic. That is what we meant too. From that there will come a hybrid, if it pleases God, that will have all that you recognize as good in you. . . . I said long ago that when one has made all the Protestants Catholic, one will find that the Catholics have become Protestant."

2
The Adaptation of the Religious Orders to the Modern World

Leibniz reflected on the notion of *religious order*; he sought the conditions of a perfect adaptation of these orders to their end, which is in his eyes a more efficacious realization of the divine plan. Leibniz' idea was to retain from each order what was best in it, then to integrate this best into a more comprehensive order. It was, at the same time, to make each of the existing orders (those, at least, whose institution was ancient) benefit from the modern spirit, which was a spirit of reason and science. Leibniz dreamed of a Church in which the Cistercians would *also* be naturalists, in which the mendicant orders would also be doctors, in which the learned orders would also be historians, the missionaries also linguists, the contemplatives also mathematicians, the theologians also critics, the liturgists also admirers of nature and her cycles. Leibniz feared lest all the capacity of attention of the religious limit itself to their liturgical or pastoral task, such, at least, as this function had been conceived before the awakening of the sciences. Leibniz believed that the scientific conquests "are no less included than the others in the apostolic functions." It is not necessary, he wrote to Father Verjus, that "all the religious sit in the confessionals or unceasingly meditate discourses or matters of conscience." Leibniz advised a division of labor: on the one hand, the propagation of the faith by the missions, and on the other, the justification of the faith by the sciences. He even dreamed, as we were saying, of transforming the orders into *one* supreme order, order of orders, order of charity: *Instituatur Societas sive ordo caritatis, compositus ex contemplativis et activis*, order in which the pope would be chosen.

It was within the method of Leibniz, so contrary in this respect to that of Descartes, to make no innovations, but to accommodate himself to what already existed, limiting himself to grafting it into his own sap. Leibniz saw in the order of the Jesuits the religious establishment most kindred to that which he would have founded himself. He, too, was preoccupied with the "glory of God." But the Jesuits were established, and it was not necessary to found them anew: invaluable economy of effort! It could only be a question of completing, or at least of continuing, the work of Ignatius and of his first companions by infusing into it, as in infinitesimal calculation, the little difference capable of making the given present progress toward its limit and perfection. Leibniz said that he desired to take up the effort of the Jesuits where this effort had stopped: "*Alda anfangen wo die Jesuiten aufhören.*"

Leibniz was keenly aware of the transformation of minds beneath the apparent immobility of his century. Where Bossuet ruled, the opposite of Bossuet began to gain ground. And, in this new mentality, the work of reason on nature was going to take the place of the old theology, which was rather a work of reason on grace. To be sure, Pascal had celebrated the progress of the sciences; it is the moderns who for Pascal are the true ancients, because knowledge is cumulative. But Pascal, who did not suspect the transformations of structure, had not perceived that the progress of the sciences, once the human mind had clearly understood its law, would modify the thoughts of men on traditional religion and would disturb the very foundations of the social order. His *libertin* is a "free thinker," a personal enemy of God: he is not a philosopher, nor a scholar, nor one who works with his mind, nor a reformer of society. Ten years pass (little difference), and Leibniz, more attentive than Pascal to nascent things, has an inkling of the coming modifications, which cause the human mind to enter into a new era. In 1671, in a letter to Arnauld, he wrote: "The most profound religious science is today the indispensable necessity. Why? Because a philosophical century is beginning in which, by the natural and legitimate course of things, a greater concern with the truth is going to become widespread, outside of the schools, in the mind of men of all social conditions. If we cannot satisfy this need of knowledge, we have to renounce the veritable propagation of religion. Soon many more men will no longer be Christian save in appearance; evil and energetic minds will work for the ruin of the faith, and atheism and naturalism will be the last heresies." And that is why Leibniz wanted religious minds, of all degrees and in all states, to be enlightened, and scientific study to be raised from the discredit in which a false asceticism had placed it. In this respect he is quite different from Pascal who, in the last days of his life, renounced the exercise of genius so that charity might reign completely. Leibniz observed that "although one can be saved and live virtuously as well without knowing either Rabbinistics, nor history, nor mathematics, it is nevertheless of importance to the public that there be men, each of whom cultivates the one of these fields of knowledge for which he will have the most talent. . . . For it is known that these studies, these special occupations, far from hindering the practice of the Christian virtues, serve (some more directly than others) the great objective which one should set for oneself."

Pascal might have objected here that the study of the sciences can only serve salvation after the purification of the heart: thus, St. John of the Cross, after the trials of the mystic night, permits the soul, finally stripped of itself, the use of goods and even of sensible goods: man can then sublime everything, having renounced himself. On the contrary, Leibniz seems to think that the study of the sciences has by itself the virtue of elevating the soul, and that by itself it gives God his glory, in such a way that it could become the equivalent of or the substitute for religion. Leibniz would readily have said that science and piety, knowledge and prayer are one and the same act, although translated into different languages. In these conditions, technical competence becomes as important as ascetic value. There are even cases in which this competence can be more useful to the divine work, skill being less ambiguous than love. Leibniz attempts to unite the spirit of Ignatius with that of Spinoza, the inspiration of the *Exercises* with that of the *Ethics*. Let us cite here a saying of Leibniz, in a letter to Colbert, which translates this *pensée de derrière* into an admirable example: "A Chinese mandarin will be transported with astonishment when he has understood the infallibility of a missionary-geometrician."

: : :

Pascal would have been indignant here. And yet, by proposing the problem of the cycloid in order to put his excellence of mind in the service of his faith, he had employed a method which Leibniz criticized, observing that such challenges are double-edged, that Mr. Wallis in England and Mr. Laloubère in France, having found a way to solve the same problem, did "some harm to Pascal." Here, it is Leibniz who attacked the missionary geometrician.

3
The Syncretic Ecumenism of Leibniz

Placed between Catholicism and Protestantism, and eager to reconcile them, Leibniz does not choose one of the two terms in order to make the other enter into it, he does not propose an ecumenical unity into which the two religions would come, losing their identity. He attempts to push both spirits to the limit. Thus, he strives to reform Protestantism according to his ideal model by more unity among the confessions, more flexibility in its principles, more conformity to tradition in its practices, more breadth in its relations with the Catholic Church. And, at the same time, he proposes reforming Catholicism by securing the rational connection of its doctrines, their consonance with primitive times, by furnishing justification of the dogmas apparently the most inadmissible to modern men (like the resurrection and transubstantiation), by showing the appropriateness of practices in appearance corrupt (like the worship of the saints or private masses), finally by offering plans of reform for the religious orders and giving directives concerning the mission of the Church in the world. Doing this, he pleases (so he believes, at least) both parties. Besides diminishing by infinitely small quantities several misunderstandings about details, he prepares to the limit a union which will ask neither of the opposing parties to abjure its faith. Thus one progresses toward the ideal Church, where the present Churches find themselves "more noble than in themselves." And, the reunion once accomplished, the differences which would still remain by the weight of the past and its indistinct perception would tend to disappear, as do the differences in the calculation of the infinite.

"You are right," Leibniz wrote to Mme de Brinon, "to say that, in the way in which we are going about it, it seems that the Catholics would all become also Protestant and that the Protestants would become Catholic. That is what we meant too. From that there will come a hybrid, if it pleases God, that will have all that you recognize as good in you. . . . I said long ago that when one has made all the Protestants Catholic, one will find that the Catholics have become Protestants."

In short, Leibniz' idea was to consider Catholicism and Protestantism two contradictory terms which it was a matter of uniting by asking each one to be faithful to the last to its essence.

The center of gravity is in the beyond of the future, at the extreme limit of the progression. If we apply these thoughts to the understanding of religion, our perspectives are going to change. The religious institution, too, sees itself considered under this aspect of infinite progression. Its point of origin, in which it tended to see its essence, becomes merely a point of departure, analogous to the first term in a series of numbers. The custom of an early era which we call *tradition* would not be able to govern forever a movement which entails the infinite. If Leibniz does not speak this language to Bossuet (which Bossuet, so little versed in metaphysics, would not have understood), it is nonetheless this thought which inspires him at all times in his long correspondence. Leibniz conceives each element of religion as a moment in a transition; revelation is not completed, ecumenicity is not constituted, definitions are not definitive.

On many points Leibniz is in advance of the Catholic theologians of his time, who often answer him inadequately. For Arnauld and Bossuet deny all change; they defend a static tradition, whereas in order to follow Leibniz into his domain and combat him with his own weapons, it would have been necessary to ask him for a more profound analysis of the notion of change in the matter of faith. But, as Descartes observed in the *Discourses*, "the action by which one knows a thing is different from that by which one knows that one believes it." In the seventeenth century the Catholic theologians were behind living Catholicism, their thoughts were less rich than the permanent object of these thoughts.

Leibniz, when he places himself in the Catholic perspective, is perfectly aware of what Catholicism presupposes: the Church, in order to explain herself to herself, must admit that, without adding to the faith, she has the power to "analyze it with the assistance of the Holy Spirit," that this analysis is not limited to a logical process by which one would extract from the faith heretofore defined what was necessarily contained therein.[3] Without possessing the notion of *development* (which will only become classic two centuries after him), Leibniz provides several of its elements. One readily imagines a correspondence between Leibniz and a disciple of Newman, analogous to that which Leibniz had had with Père des Bosses, in which Leibniz would have shown the harmony of "development" with his own system, as he had shown the harmony of "transubstantiation with his principles." But it would have been an entirely different development than that which Catholic thought admits to explain the history of dogma. Indeed, in the latest philosophy of Leibniz at least, the development which he would have admitted would hardly have differed from Hegelian "becoming," in the sense that this develop-

[3] "It seems that you yourself, Monseigneur, leave some backdoor open by saying that the ecumenical councils, when they decide some truth, do not propose any new dogmas, but merely declare those which have always been believed and explain them simply in clearer and more precise terms. For if the declaration contains any proposition which cannot be drawn by a legitimate and certain consequence from what was already received beforehand, and is therefore not virtually included therein, it will be necessary to admit that the new decision does indeed establish a new article, although one would like to hide the thing under the name of a declaration." May 14, 1700; Foucher de Careil, II, 231.

ment would have been conceived not as the explanation of a virtual given, but as the tendency of the essence of the dogma toward a better and undetermined state. Moreover, as far as the facts are concerned, Leibniz would not have agreed that there had been no authentic development but in the single Roman Catholic line. History would not have seem to him to testify in this direction. His conception of being did not lead him to privilege one monad.[4]

If there had been development, it would thus have been everywhere and at all times. Regular development would not have been peculiar to the Church; one would have observed it in all the confessions: it would have been common to all the monads. It would have been a metaphysical law and not an improbable accident.

Leibniz makes an effort to place himself above the disagreement, in order to reconcile the Roman conception of unity around the one Rome with the "comprehensive" conception of the union of the churches. But here again the intermediary that he proposes is on only one of the two slopes: he remains more ecumenical than Catholic.

[4] There would nevertheless be a way to explain the Roman position in his system: it would be to see in the Catholic development a complete monad, and in the other lines of duration, monads incomplete and confused owing to the excessive prevalence of one of their elements. In this case (and in order to make use of analogies loved by Leibniz) the relationship of the ellipse to the parabola could represent the relationship of Catholicism to the confessions issued from it—the parabola being an ellipse whose focus, wrested from its equilibrium, finds itself carried out to the infinite.

For, in a Catholic way of thought, historic universality cannot be considered one of two contradictory terms, which it would be necessary to unite with Protestant inferiority in order to make up a richer essence. The *raison d'être* of the Catholic Church is to affirm that she is unique, that is, if we translate this reflection into the language of ontology, that she possesses the structure of being and the composition of contradictory terms. She does not have to borrow elsewhere, nor to expect from the future a complement of essence. And, to be sure, it is possible that, in consequence of rhythms of time, by the effect of circumstances or by the prevalence of some influence, one of the two contradictory terms has appeared to be, in her, alone admitted. One cannot deny that there have been periods in which the Church has put more emphasis on grace than on freedom, or on the authority of the pope than on that of the bishops; it is even possible that, for long periods, one of the contradictory terms is obscured or not yet developed. It has, nonetheless, a virtual existence: if an exterior influence were necessary in order to make it appear, it would limit itself to calling it forth: it would not create it. It is this point that Leibniz can scarcely understand. If Catholic intransigence seems to him to be intolerance it is because he admits the Catholic value and the Protestant value at the same time. Moreover, if the philosopher in him had to choose, it is the Protestant value that he would prefer, as being the purer or, rather, the only pure value, the only value truly universal and worthy of the mind.

4
The Justification of Nonconversion

Leibniz was perfectly aware that *from the point of view of Catholics,* where his method of justice and of love made him place himself, he was not on the legitimate path of salvation. And, with his subtile perspicacity, he attempted to show sometimes that the Catholics were mistaken, sometimes that in the case where the Protestants would be in error, since this error was from the Catholic point of view irrefutable, he was justified in remaining Protestant.

A strange thing: Leibniz was anxious to be a true Catholic, in spite of his outward remoteness. He wrote to Mme de Brinon: "You are right, Madame, to judge me Catholic at heart. And I am so even openly: for there is but obstinacy that makes the heretic; and of that, thank God, my conscience does not accuse me." He acknowledged himself a member of the Church by the communion of charity in Jesus Christ. He went even further, judging this first condition insufficient if he did not make every endeavor to be also a member of the outward communion of the Church "visible and recognizable by the continual succession of her hierarchy." Let us acknowledge that it is difficult for a non-Catholic to go further in good will: the attitude of Leibniz prefigures that of Soloviev in the Russian Church, of Lord Halifax in the Anglican Church, of Bergson and Simone Weil in Judaism. Leibniz is persuaded that, in the state of the Roman Church, several of the philosophical opinions to which he is attached in conscience and which he can thus not renounce without moral error, would not be accepted by Roman authority: he would thus be considered outside the Church, just at the moment when he would enter it. He likens his case to the situation of a Catholic who would find himself unjustly excommunicated and who would not fail to desire outward communion with all his strength.

He is interested in persons who have been declared heretics owing to a factual error, of whom St. Augustine says that God will crown them in secret.[5]

"Nevertheless, these persons believe themselves to be true Catholics, as would be those whom one has unjustly excommunicated, *clave errante*, for they hold the dogmas of the Catholic Church, they wish in addition the outward communion, to which others place obstacles or refuse it to them."

But despite this effort, which I believe sincere in the last analysis, Leibniz remains in the universe of pure freedom.

It is in his correspondence with Mme de Brinon, whose feminine mind goes straight to the essence, that Leibniz comes more and more to light: it is there that one rediscovers the eternal dialogue of contradictory terms, and the same accusation of obstinacy thrown from one to the other; Pascal would surely have spoken like Mme de Brinon: "The truth does not come in two; either you are mistaken or we are mistaken: the latter could not be since we have not

[5] This case was pointed out by St. Augustine, *De vera religione*, II: *Hos coronat in occulto Pater, in occulto videns: rarum hoc videtur genus sed tamen exempla no desunt: imo plura sunt quam credi potest.*

broken the union and since we have remained attached to the thick of the tree."

To which Leibniz replied: "You say that it is necessary to be attached to the thick of the tree, but the thick of the tree is Jesus Christ; he is the vine, we are its branches. Judge whether those whose devotions are solid and go to God himself are not more attached to it than those who throw themselves into superstitious practices and give to creatures what belongs but to God alone, who himself claims to be so jealous of his glory.

"It is necessary to work with fervor to correct those whom one finds in error, and when the hope to do so is lost, it is necessary to break openly with those who disfigure the Church of God; otherwise one takes part in their damnation, by closing one's eyes on these public abuses."

5
Difference with Pascal

It is here that it is good to evoke that genius related to that of Leibniz, and which had inspired him in his mathematical discoveries: Pascal. They resemble one another and they differ profoundly. Pascal would be a protester in temperament but Catholic in thought and faith. Leibniz, on the contrary, so Protestant in the substance of his thought, has an ecumenical and, one can almost say, Catholic temperament: he feels very close to the Jesuit fathers so roughly handled by Pascal.

Pascal and Leibniz participate, in differing degrees, in

the religious crisis opened in the sixteenth century by the Reformation: one belongs to the Roman religion; the other is a Lutheran.

In neither case was it an external adherence. They had thought, each of them, of departing from their orthodoxy; they had asked themselves the anxious question of the Christian: *Can I find salvation here?* Pascal had been tempted to leave the visible communion of the Roman Church; he had declined to do so only after much tribulation. Inversely, Leibniz had been entreated by princes, bishops, friends, to enter into the body of the Catholic Church; he had never consented to do so and, it seems, was less and less inclined to do so as he advanced in age. Finally, it is fitting to note that Leibniz posed to himself the problem of the union of the churches all his life, whereas Pascal in the quarrels of Jansenism was led to reflect on the unity of the Church.

: : :

A philosopher of history, when he considers the scission of Christendom, is led to wonder what its significance is in the development of the human spirit.

Does it have causes which are merely casual, accidental, like the problems posed by the reform of an organism having gone through sixteen centuries of time? Or is it necessary to look for more profound reasons for the Reformation of the sixteenth century, reasons which result from a divergence on the very *essence* of Christianity? Is one to believe that the basic elements of the religion of Jesus had not received, before Luther and Calvin, their authentic interpretation: the faith, the works, the sacraments, the priesthood, the idea of the Church and of the head of the Church? The confrontation of Leibniz and Pascal could be of assistance in the reflection on these problems. It is indeed a characteristic of these two geniuses not to have admitted of separation in their activities, outwardly so diverse. Their faith, fecundated by their thought, forms with it a unique system. That will permit us to discern what the profound metaphysics is which characterizes and which opposes Catholicism and Protestantism.

: : :

Protestant thought is *existential* in the highest degree; it considers man in his present condition. And, although it elevates God above all nature and seems not to be interested but in his glory, it is nevertheless the drama of the justification of sinful man which preoccupies it most of all, far more than the glorification of God in his works. One could object that this character of anthropocentrism is absent from Calvin, who seeks in everything the glory of God. But the "glory" of which Calvin is thinking and which he obtains is not the *universal* glory (that which bursts forth in divine mystery and in the creation), rather it is the glory which God gives himself by the predestination of men in Jesus Christ: the glory is conceived as the consequence of the salvation of men. I do not mean here that, in a Catholic way of thought, these aspects are absent, but they are subordinated to an aspect more properly *religious,* in the technical sense of the term: man refers to his Creator before referring to his Savior. The virtue of "religion" for St. Thomas is not first of all a virtue useful for salvation, but a virtue of justice, *potissima pars justitiae.*[6] God has rights on us before we have needs and demands in regard to him. One of the essential traits of the Catholic religion is thereby explained: it satisfies, without idolatry, the natural tendency of the intellect to worship. Protestantism, by diminishing this side of religion—by which Christianity continued, purifying it, the religion of the early ages and the ancient tradition—tended to restrict the virtue of piety to intimate relations of the soul with God, of sinners with the Redeemer. That is why in Protestant areas there was generally neither cathedral, nor liturgy, nor religious order, nor contemplation of praise, but above all the feeling of a drama within the soul, before God alone.

If this antithesis is basically true, there is no need to hesitate. It is Pascal who is characteristically Protestant, and Leibniz who is characteristically Catholic.

Thus Pascal, as has been shown especially by Mr. Baudin, is opposed to that theocentric conception of the universe which had been that of antiquity and the Middle Ages. He is interested above all in the inner man; he defines what the latter can lose or gain by his conduct: he does not seek God in physical nature, but much rather in the human heart. He experiences God less by his presence sensible to the heart than by the hunger he has of him. He does not

[6] IIa IIae q. 122, I; see Baudin, *Etudes historiques et critiques sur la Philosophie de Pascal,* Neuchâtel 1946-47, II, 173, 187.

admit the existence of a *natural* reason, of an *eternal* law of morals: if there were no revelation it would be reasonable for us to be libertines and to turn to pleasures. This way of looking at things amounts to binding morals to the faith, contrary to the teaching of the ancients, who saw in moral action the work of reason and of nature. One understands also that Pascal was able to condemn science, the arts, philosophy as vanity. For him, deism is almost as far removed from the Christian religion as atheism. "All those," he says, "who seek God outside of Jesus Christ and who come to a standstill in nature, either find no light which satisfies them, or manage to make for themselves a means of knowing God and of serving him without a mediator, and they thereby fall either into atheism or into deism, which are two things which the Christian religion abhors almost equally."[7] God sometimes remains, in Pascal, the jealous God of the Old Testament, who enlightens and who blinds; the love of God and the hate of oneself are correlative.

No Protestant thinker has penetrated more than Leibniz the spirit of the Society of Jesus; none has shown more affinity with the Jesuit spirit, none has better pleaded the case of the Jesuits, which is still open. He understood them on certain points better than they understood themselves at that time. He was faithful to his method, which was to help the others be faithful to the last to their own essence,

[7] *Pensées* no. 556 (no. 449).

even, indeed, to suggest to them the means of surpassing themselves in their own line. And if a reformer of the celebrated Society felt one day the need to rejuvenate it in accordance with its character, he would still find in this friendly outside observer some useful indications.

In this respect, Leibniz is quite different from Pascal. From the beginning Pascal knew the Jesuits from the outside; he was immediately carried away by polemics; he saw but one aspect of this great body. If he *characterized* the Jesuit, it was as Molière was able to do so, with the gifts of the comedian who sees roughly and who composes the machine to make people laugh. Pascal thought he detected in the Jesuit spirit the most subtile corruption of the Christian spirit: charity diverted from its aim and translated into the justification of evil; in short, that sin against the spirit which has no remission. And his arguments against "Jesuitism" are strangely similar to those which Protestants use against Romanism, with this difference, that Pascal is Catholic and points out, within Troy, this enemy apparatus.

For Leibniz, it is just the opposite. The institution of the Jesuits, far from representing in his eyes the most perfidious opposition to the spirit of Christianity and to the thought of early times, is the most remarkable development of this thought, and of this original Christianity. Their faults, as serious as they might be, are accidental. The essence of the order is good. And if this order were reformed in accordance with this essence, it could procure for the Gospel the means which are at the measure of modern men, in the twofold inner and outer mission.

Leibniz, although he was born into the Confession of Augsburg, does not seem to have been profoundly affected by the Lutheran spirit. It is probably because his faith was mediocre, because he had taken very quickly to the school of the ancients, because the atmosphere of the courts had opened his mind to the affairs of the world in which the darkness of life is masked by appearances, because, finally, there had never been *for him* any problem of sin or of salvation. Leibniz represents for us fairly well what the human mind would have been if the suture had been made easily (and without the intervention of Christ) between the "science" of the moderns and the "reason" of the ancients. It is not individual salvation that he places at the end of human endeavor, but conformity to the order, to the "general good," to the "universal good." In the same spirit, he admires the physical universe, which offers us the marvels of divine wisdom; he proposes analyzing the bodies which compose it in order to see how they can be of service to our preservation and even to our greater perfection. The arts must also be cultivated, in particular music, that beautiful occupation which uplifts the soul by entering into an imitation of that universal harmony which God has put into the world. Everything helps us to further know God and in some way to augment his glory. Nothing is to be despised, but everything is to be loved and referred to God. By all these traits, Leibniz seems closer to the root idea of the Christian religion, which is to *recapitulate all things in Jesus Christ*, as St. Paul said. There exists in him a complacency for what God does, because everything that he does turns to his glory.

: : :

It has been said that Jansenism is the homologue of Protestantism in the bosom of the Church; it is, says Cournot, an "attenuated reproduction of the pattern of the Protestant Reformation."[8] In each case we find the idea of restoring the Christianity of early times, the emphasis on the part of God in the work of salvation, the super-eminent authority given to St. Augustine, the independence of private judgment, the part given to the layman in the defense of the faith and in the apostolate. But none of these traits is specifically Protestant: the Franciscans also wanted to return to the Gospel, the Thomists were very close to assenting to the formulas of St. Augustine. St. Bernard treated the pope with independence, as Paul had "resisted" Peter. The "laity" was to take an increasingly important part in the Church . . . Moreover, Port-Royal was strictly faithful to the Catholic faith in regard to the sacraments, the priesthood, the Church, even the authority of the bishops, and that of the Roman see. It is too often forgotten that the Jansenists and their time were the adversaries of the Protestants, that they rejected the idea of schism. Even if Port-Royal was destroyed, it considered itself the old guard of the Church, though grumbling.

[8] *Considérations sur la marche des idées et des événements dans les temps modernes*, Paris 1934, I, 305.

Pascal's protest is in the accent, more than in the substance. It is said that Jansenism had distorted and hardened Pascal, that it is a shame that Pascal did not meet along the way a St. Francis of Sales, or a Bérulle, and that he lived in a sort of Catholic dissidence. But how would a genius with need of *signs* and quarrels have awakened to the problems posed by religion if the latter had not appeared to him in an insolent and provoking aspect? In order to conceive, Pascal had need of an atmosphere of battle, of protest and of challenge. Even in physics, he was never more at ease than when he had contradictors. The people who knew him have told us that he always looked like a man in anger. In order for Christianity to interest him, it had to be presented in the forms in which it had appeared in the beginning: as a paradox to defend, a testimony to furnish, a struggle to revictual, an orthodoxy to support. Newman said that the first Christians formed the "party" of Jesus. Pascal would readily have joined such a party, as St. Paul did; and, just as St. Paul, once a Christian, felt rise again within him the need to do battle and exercised it upon the interior enemy constituted at that time by the "Judaizers," so Pascal, converted to a more living Christianity but not being able to cease striking out, found in the Jesuits, the Molinists and the lax the object for his indispensable anger.

Leibniz has several traits of a Germanic pattern of thought: the concern for total synthesis, the idea of an indefinite state of flux which permits being both contradictory terms at once, the supposed connection between the free and the fateful, the sense of catastrophe and resurrection which makes the recourse to the abyss a moment of reasonable conduct, and the worst a necessary moment of the best. Leibniz carries on Eckhart and Boehme, as he announces Hegel and Schelling.

There is also some Slavic blood in Leibniz. Leibniz liked to make it known. The name which he bore was, according to him, of Slavic origin (*Leubniziorum sive Lubeniecziorum slavonicum*); and at Torgau, at the time of his interview with Peter the Great, Leibniz said to the Czar: "Our origin is the same: both Slavs, you have conquered from barbarism the greatest empire of the world: as for me, I have founded by science a no less vast realm. Both initiators of new centuries, we are both of that race whose destinies no one can predict." The temperament of Leibniz makes us see this affinity of the Germanic and the Slavic which has probably not finished worrying Europe: in both cases, an extreme capacity for changes, an *amor fati* which transcends the difference of good and evil, which even sees in sin a means of approach toward God: the contempt for what unfolds in time, the carrying forward to the final end, to that eschatological moment when God will be vindicated of evil and will be everything in us. One can wonder whether Leibniz is not at bottom more an eschatologist than a philosopher of becoming. His method pushed him to place himself at the summit of the pyramid of time, that is, at the consummation of history. He is thereby more Greek Christian than Latin Christian, if it is true that the Eastern Church is more inclined to see time assumed into the eternal than to discern the operation of the eternal in time. Such a Slavism is not hostile to Germanism; on the contrary, it confirms it, since it permits justifying the opposition of contradictory terms, which then appears as provisional, a mere aspect of the midst of time. It is necessary to help, says Leibniz, the individuals capable of hastening human evolution. The idea that one must force the movement of history, accelerate it by conquests or inventions, accomplish in ten years sometimes more than in ten centuries and thus precipitate the flow of all things toward their perfection, be it by catastrophes, this is indeed a way of thought related to the Germanic genius and the Russian genius at the same time.

Leibniz is a German intelligence of Slavic *ferment*, of French *culture*; in this sense, he is European. And he represents, before Goethe and perhaps more than him, the type of what Germany could have but has not yet been.

Leibniz thus belongs to the European East and Pascal to the West of this peninsula whose mass is Asiatic.

2 Actuality of Newman

In Memory of Pierre Frieden

1
The Development of the Church

An Essay on the Development of Christian Doctrine, published in 1845, is the statement of the intellectual, philosophical and historical motives which, after long reflection, induced John Henry Newman to leave the Anglican Church, of which he was the pride, in order to reach the Roman Church, which he did not know well, which he had suspected and combatted, and in which nothing attracted him. It is rare to meet with such books. Accounts of conversion are not lacking; but often the conversions, like that of St. Augustine, are passages from a loose life to a pure life, or sudden changes in consequence of an illumination. Here it is a question of a reasonable and slow progression, having its principle in the examination of the history of the Church: the work is carried on and comes to an end in intellectual enlightenment. For this reason, the *Essay* can be of interest to philosophy, and particularly that philosophy, that theology of history which are held in such high esteem in our time.

The book and the conversion of Newman are of singular importance in the history of western religious ideas. Let us note that Newman, persuaded that the Roman Church *is* the true *development* of the Gospel and of antiquity, converted in that month of October 1845, in which the young Renan left the Seminary of Saint-Sulpice because he was not able to reconcile the faith with the Hegelian conceptions of *evolution*. The diametrical opposition of these two intellectual destinies, the ambiguity, so hidden and so profound, of the notion of "change," suggest subjects of reflection almost indispensable to anyone who wants to understand the present age and the division of doctrines.

But Newman's conversion assumes a more remarkable importance in the religious sphere. It must be remembered that, toward the middle of the last century, for observers extraneous to the faith but attentive to indices, the Catholic Church seemed to be a Church grown old and corrupt, left behind in any case by the "progress of the Enlightenment." It is the Reformation which had inspired the new philosophies, and it has been said that Kantianism was a secularized Lutheranism. Now, Newman's conversion, because of its motives, appears, according to a Protestant thinker, like "the return of the Roman Church into her intellectual rights." It announces a possible reform of the Reformation, a possible critique of the critique, and the eventuality of a return to unity. One hundred years have passed since this event of 1845, which went almost unnoticed among Catholics, which was generally kept quiet in the Protestant world. And one can already measure the contribution of Newman to theology for the treatise *De Ecclesia*. It can be said that Newman gave to the Church the intellectual instrument which she needs in order to understand her temporal development, her passage in time, and something like a "note," until then almost unprecedented, of her truth.

It must be noted that this *Essay* is not directly accessible to the Latin and French spirit. One finds there a singular disparity between the richness of the intuition which animates it and the demonstrations which Newman gives of this intuition. Such is the characteristic of works written in the glow of discovery, before inspiration has come to rest. The work also bears the stigma of interruption. It resembles those posthumous books, unfinished because of the death of the author and published by his heirs. It suffers from the haste with which it was written. It is not made for a mind accustomed to precise definitions. And one understands the irritation of the Roman theologians—as surprised by the form as by the content—one of whom said: *Newman miscet et confundit omnia.*[1]

Another thing which makes access to this work difficult is that it has two fields, two aims, and that the adapta-

[1] *La Philosophie de Newman,* Paris 1933, XVI. We refer occasionally to our book, *La Philosophie de Newman,* under the abbreviation *P.N.*, and to *Renan et Newman,* Aix 1938, under the abbreviation *R.N.*

tion of the inner eye is effected with difficulty. It responds to two problems; it aims at two types of adversaries; it polemizes on two fronts.

The first of these problems is a Christian, ecclesiological problem: it refers to the quarrel of Roman Catholics and Protestants or Orthodox.

The second of these problems is more vast, more metaphysical: it concerns *being and time*.

The first of these problems is connected with a treatise *De Ecclesia*, the second with a treatise *De Ente, De Genesi* . . . or further, with a *De Natura Rerum*.

The first of these polemics is an anti-Protestant, anti-Anglican polemic. The second is an anti-Spencerian, anti-Hegelian polemic. The first, placed in this moment, would be anti-Barthian, the second, anti-Marxist.

But the result of this duality of aims (the one explicit, too explicit—the other implicit, too implicit) is that the work meets rarely with its true reader. Those who are concerned with theology are disconcerted, because Newman does not speak the language of theologians. Those who are philosophers or metaphysicians are repelled, because they find neither the problems, nor the method, nor the language of philosophy.[2]

My present reflection is directed toward diminishing these difficulties by raising the intelligence above the division of these two problems.

[2] One could say further that, among theologians, the Anglicans considered the work confused, biased. The Roman theologians accepted the conclusions, but not the premises.

2
The Thought of Newman

❪ 1

Newman considers human history in its widest signification. He describes it without any presupposition. He remarks that everything takes place as if human history were the field of operation of what he calls the "idea" . . . a word which it has always been a delicate matter to define in all languages, and particularly in the English language, in which *idea* is closer to *image* than to *essence* or *form*.

The Newmanian idea is an essence, a structure, a form—but incarnate in temporal matter. This essence then manifests itself in an individual consciousness in the form of an intuition, or rather of a project. But very quickly, it is expressed either by a *doctrine* or by an *institution*. Examples are abundant, for each historic reality can be considered as an Idea. Christianity and all its diversities, its heresies, its parties, its movements, its dogmas, its theological systems, its liturgies, its organs of government and of control are so many "Ideas." This is a first privileged field of experience. Newman knows it better than any other, either for having studied it in one of its characteristic moments, the fourth century, in his essay on *The Arians*, or for having himself been the agent of one of these "Ideas" at the time of the Oxford movement and in the campaign of the Tracts. But one could apply this method of historical analysis (fairly closely related to the monadology of Leibniz) to all temporal existence. And, for example, nowadays one could study, as so many "Ideas" at work in time: communism, surrealism, phenomenology, ecumenism, the European community, or even Newmanism . . .

Newman put stress on the disparity between the "Idea" and its expressions, which are signs. This disparity is analogous to that which exists between the unity and the sum of its parts in the argument of Zeno or in infinitesimal calculus: $1 = \frac{1}{2} + \frac{1}{4} + \frac{1}{8} + \ldots$ The "Idea" for Newman is the sum of all the experiences which one can have of it, of all the expressions which one can give to it, of all the consequences which one can draw from it. And that is why the Idea needs TIME in order to make its successive aspects appear, the multiplicity of formulas not being able to equal the simplicity of the object which they intend to express. A curious notion, which one will find again in a certain way in Bergson, who had read Newman.

⁅ 2

Up until this point we have been in the climate of Platonism. But it is intimately modified by the belief in the incarnation of the Word. The "Ideas" of Newman are not intemporal models which are degraded by being compounded with passive and disorderly matter. They become incarnate in historic existences, they animate personal beings or structures composed of persons. We are far from Plato.

We will be still further from him when we have said that the "Ideas," in Newman, are in competition. They are subject to the laws of growth and corruption. This is the dramatic side of Newman's thought, in which one senses the influence of his milieu, of his moment and of his race. He writes at the time when Darwin is speaking of "vital competition" and "struggle for life." He belongs to that realist, mystic, pragmatic race of Britons, so interested by action, struggle, effectiveness.

The Ideas are at work. They are not themselves their own essence. They are not necessarily conformable to their patterns. And one can even say that, the occasions of infidelity to the essence being multiplied with the temporal situations in which they find themselves placed, there exists an always growing number of chances of alienation and alteration.

"But whatever be the risk of corruption from intercourse with the world around, such a risk must be encountered if a great idea is duly to be understood, and much more if it is to be fully exhibited. It is elicited and expanded by trial, and battles into perfection and supremacy. Nor does it escape the collision of opinion even in its earlier years, nor does it remain truer to itself, and with a better claim to be considered one and the same, though externally protected from vicissitude and change. It is indeed sometimes said that the stream is clearest near the spring. Whatever use may fairly be made of this image, it does not apply to the history of a philosophy or belief, which on the contrary is more equable, and purer, and stronger when its bed has become deep, and broad, and full. It necessarily rises out of an existing state of things, and for a time savors of the soil. Its vital element needs disengaging from what is foreign and temporary, and is employed in efforts after freedom which become more vigorous and hopeful as its years increase. Its beginnings are no measure of its capabilities, nor its scope. At first no one knows what it is, or what it is worth. It remains perhaps for a time quiescent; it tries, as it were, its limbs, and proves the ground under it, and feels its way. From time to time it makes essays which fail, and are in consequence abandoned. It seems in suspense which way to go; it wavers, and at length strikes out in one definite direction. In time it enters upon strange territory; points of controversy alter their bearing; parties rise and fall around it; dangers and hopes appear in new relations; and old principles reappear under new forms. It changes with them in order to remain the same. In a higher world it is otherwise, but here below to live is to change, and to be perfect is to have changed often."[3]

3

Up to now Newman had limited himself to exposition. But this description put him on the track of a Logic. He was led to seek the criteria which would permit distinguishing between the realization of an Idea which is true to the essence of the Idea, and that which is foreign or contrary to it. Newman therefore established a series of signs or "notes," distinguishing the Pure from the Impure.

Newman chose seven criteria, probably guided by the seven criteria of falseness which, in his youth, his master

[3] *An Essay on the Development of Christian Doctrine,* ch. I, sect. 1, §7; see *P.N.*, 86.

Whately had proposed to him to illustrate the errors of Roman Catholicism. It is evident that this division by seven is rather arbitrary, and even more evident that Newman did not develop equally the seven notes which he proposed, which are: continuity of principles, power of assimilation, logical sequence, anticipation of the future, conservative action upon the past, and chronic vigor.

One could maintain that there exist two series of "notes," those which are notes of permanence, and those which are notes of growth, it being well understood that the latter are subordinant to the former, for growth should take place with a view to preserving the permanence. One could further say that the former notes concern the static identity of the *Structure*, and the latter the dynamic identity of Progress, progress and structure being the two elements of *Development*.

The note which Newman set forth, illustrated and defined at greatest length is that which corresponds to the zone of experience into which he had gone most deeply, namely the history of patristic times.

This note consists in what one could call the equivalence of the aspects of an Idea or more exactly of the *proportion of these aspects throughout the disparity of situations, of ages and of circumstances.* The best comparison (which is not to be found, I believe, in Newman) would be that of the human visage. One fixes the visage at various periods of life, one compares these snapshot outlines, and one then says that the person resembles himself, that it is the *same* person. One *recognizes* him (*reconnaître*) which is different, and perhaps more, than to know him (*connaître*). It is not a question of a photographically exact identity, but of an analogy of the depths. Newman notes that there exist portraits which sometimes disconcert us, but which we finally judge more exact than those too scrupulous images which are almost caricatures. Inversely, he alludes to those cases in which the same mask remains, despite a radical change: thus, he says, when the Roman republic becomes an empire.

"Next, I have a clear perception, clearer and clearer as my own experience of existing religions increases, and such as every one will share with me, who carefully examines the matter, that this ethical system (ἦθος we used to call it at Oxford as realized in individuals) is the living principle also of present Catholicism, and not of any form of Protestantism whatever—living, both as to its essential life, and also as being its vigourous motive power. . . . Outward circumstances or conditions of its presence may change or not; the Pope may be a subject one day, a sovereign another; *primus inter pares* in early times, the *episcopus episcoporum* now; there might be no devotions to the Blessed Virgin formerly, they may be superabundant of late; the Holy Eucharist might be a bare commemoration in the first century, and is a sacrifice in the nineteenth (of course I have my own definite and precise convictions of these points, but they are nothing to the purpose here, when I want to confine myself to patent facts which no one ought to dispute); but I say, even supposing there have been changes in doctrine and policy, still the *ethos* of the Catholic Church is what it was of old time, and whatever and whoever quarrels with Catholicism now, quarrels virtually, and would have quarreled, if alive 1800 years ago, with the Christianity of Apostles and Evangelists."[4]

We are now capable of understanding the basis of the argument which led Newman to convert.

It is an argument of logic, of coherence, of fidelity of the mind to itself.

One could represent by this diagram the force of the

[4] Letter of December 3, 1875 to John R. Mozley published in the *Contemporary Review* of September 1899, 367-370, cited in *P.N.*, 113. Newman is not afraid in the *Essay* to point out the errors of certain pre-Nicean fathers: their theological writings occasionally contain imprecise suggestions, incomplete openings, which will later give birth to heresies. But the inverse is equally true: certain heresies contain doctrines, principles and institutions which will later become orthodox. There is nothing more remarkable in this respect, for Newman, than the analysis of the Montanist movement. He recalls the rigorous fasts of the Montanists, the value which they attach to celibacy and to martyrdom, their scorn of temporal possessions, their penitential discipline, their idea of a center of unity. Now, the doctrinal precisions and the ecclesiastical usages of the Middle Ages are the veritable fulfillments of these prefigurations. Thus the prophets of Montanism prefigure the doctors of the Church; their inspiration, her infallibility; their revelations, her development, and Montanus himself could be considered as the (unpleasant) anticipation of the saint of Assisi. Finally, it is in the Montanist works of Tertullian that it is necessary to search for the first expression of dogmatic development. Likewise in the Novatians, Newman will further say, we discern the aspirations of nature to those pure creations of grace which are a St. Benedict or a St. Bruno. Likewise again, the effort of Sabellius to explain the divine unity was not to lead but to St. Augustine.

reasoning by means of which Newman constrains himself to be consistent with himself.

The block ABCD represents antiquity. The triangle EBF represents the "Roman corruptions" in the eyes of the early Newman. The triangle BCD represents the developments of the ancient Church, particularly that of Nicea, whose legitimacy Newman admits. The line CBE represents the continued development of the Church on the Roman Catholic axis, to which Newman gives his assent in 1845.

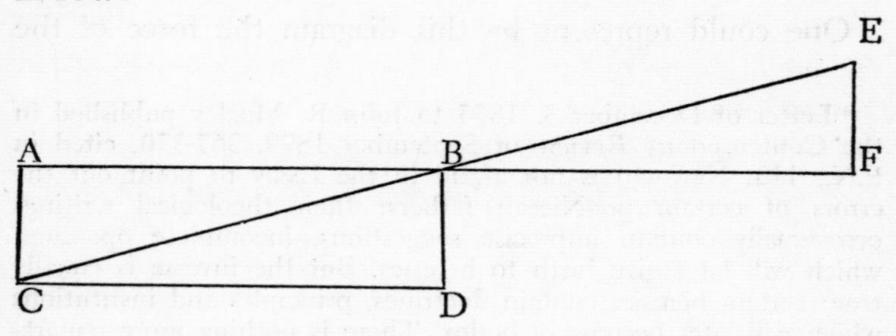

He who admits the faith of the first centuries (CDB) and who rejects the Roman definitions (EBF) is illogical: one must accept the whole or reject the whole, but not remain betwixt and between.

One example was particularly dear to Newman, that of the choice by the Council of Nicea of the word ὁμοούσιος (*consubstantialis*), in order to define the dogma of the Trinity against Arius. Newman showed that which Karl Barth, one hundred years later, was to perceive in his turn, that ὁμοούσιος of Nicea, although it was a new, equivocal term, imposed by the imperial power, had nevertheless become in fact an exact, clear, distinct, legitimate term, indispensable for defining the faith against the Arians, and which "in its folly, was more true than all the wisdom which was opposed to it."[5]

But while Karl Barth, with the Protestant tradition and the early Newman of 1833, although justifying the addition of ὁμοούσιος to the Credo and the first "development" of Nicea, rejects the legitimacy of the "developments" of the councils of Trent and of the Vatican and of dogma like purgatory, the Immaculate Conception, infallibility—the Newman of 1845 sees no valid reason for not also admitting the later developments—which were defined by the Church against innovators in a way analogous to that of Nicea, of Ephesus and of Constantinople. The whole problem consists in knowing whether the word "analogous" is appropriate here.[6]

[5] The words in quotation marks are those of Karl Barth, in his *Dogmatik*, volume II, part one. Let us recall here that in 264 a council held at Antioch to condemn Paul of Samosata had repudiated the term ὁμοούσιος, which was not scriptural, and which could have a materialistic meaning. Newman often came back to this point. See the texts in my book *P.N.*, 17 and 154. Karl Barth further recognizes that "it is finally by remaining faithful to this formula that the Church has succeeded in giving a sufficiently clear expression to her entire thought," that "all the lines of our reflection on the divinity of Christ lead us finally to the point where we can but justify the dogma."

The expression of Karl Barth could also be applied, in our opinion, to the definitions concerning the sacraments, the primacy, the Marian dogmas.

[6] Concerning these problems, see the work which Père J. H. Walgrave has consecrated to Newman, *Newman, le développement du Dogme*, Paris 1956.

But at the same time as by this *positive argument,* Newman was also guided by a *negative argument,* based on the analogy between the position of the Anglican Church in relation to the Roman Church and the position of the sects which he considered at that time as schismatic. Donatism, and in particular Semi-Arianism, seemed to him to be the first figures of a "median Church," based on the authorities, *literally* faithful to the origin, but congealed, and holding the Roman Church for "corrupt."

From then on, the equation of the past and the present was complete for the positive and negative qualities. And in 1848 Newman was able to write:

"I saw in the Semi-Arians the Via-medians; I saw in the Catholic Church of the day the identical self of the Catholic Church now; —as you know a friend by his words and deeds, or see an author in his works."[7]

[7] Letter to Wilberforce, 1848, in W. Ward, *Life of John Henry Cardinal Newman,* I, 616. One could find many indications in the work of Newman concerning these historic researches dealing with development, which he has *seeded* in his writings—giving to the word "seed" its sense of profusion, of apparent negligence, of confidence in divine chance, which will make certain seeds sprout and let others suffocate. Let it suffice to note, slightly at random, the extremely fruitful suggestions concerning the history of the Jewish religion and the prophetic books, the adoration of the saints, the development of penitence, that of purgatory, the primacy, infallibility—and concerning the mariological development, whose scope he justified and limited, showing that he drew the implicit consequences from the *Theotokos,* which was itself implied in the Gospel (see *P.N.,* 106-108, 111, 128, 129, 136). In the nineteenth century, Newman is the *Doctor Marianus* par excellence, in the sense that he does not repeat that which has already been said by theologians and mystics regarding the Virgin

3
The Thought of Newman and the Theology of the Church

It can be said that the implicit philosophy of Newman is more intelligible for us than in his time, that it has been more deeply fathomed since philosophy has meditated on the *Instant,* following Kierkegaard and in the wake of Protestant thought.

1

It is indeed a theme which Protestant thought (to the extent to which it attempts to determine its implicit theses) had necessarily to come up against. One can define Protestantism in several ways: thus, by its ecclesiology, by its doctrine of justification, by its conception of grace and of that which results from it; one will always find anew the idea that the communication of the divine gift to man (that "news" which the Gospel announces) takes place in Christ *alone,* by Christ *alone,* by faith *alone,* by God *alone*—the word "alone" (like the Greek *μόνος* in the expression *mono*theism) excluding absolutely all *real* competition of nature, of merit, of institution, of temporality. And from that point on, although many Protestants admit a visible institution, a sacramental system—grace, gift, salvation do not have their necessary condition in the adherence

Mary, but adds a new element of intelligibility and piety, by linking the development of the idea of Christ and of the Church. I tried to place myself in his footsteps when I wrote my book on the *Vierge Marie,* Paris 1950.

of the faithful to a visible, hierarchical society. This means that if there is an historic institution, it is not divinely guaranteed, if there is a priesthood, it is not visible. Karl Barth seems to have deduced, or rather to have induced for us on this point, with a radical vigor—more radical than that of Luther and Calvin—the presupposed fundamental of Protestantism, considered in its purest aspect.

Now, if I attempt to define that which derives from this first postulate, in regard to the conception of time, I will say this:

The time of a Christian life inserted into the Church cannot be justified, any more than the divine character of this Church. If, for the Protestants, the communication of grace is temporal, if the design of the people of God is carried on after Jesus, if the Church is a continuation of Israel, there is nevertheless after Jesus, in time, no normative axis. Grace is given by a direct path, perpendicular —if one may say so—to time, by a succession of secret, instantaneous visits, and not by the participation in a society which continues and develops in fact the initial Christ.[8]

This amounts to saying that in Protestantism, eternity

[8] It is true that Kierkegaard, when he spoke of the Instant of Christ, wanted above all to oppose Hegel and Hegelian becoming, which rendered Christianity unthinkable, because it rejected any privileged moment. And in his critique of Hegel, Kierkegaard did not speak as a Protestant, but as a Christian. But when the thought of Kierkegaard was rediscovered in the Protestant milieux at the beginning of the twentieth century, the Instant then assumed an eminent value.

passes into time not by the duration, but rather in and by the instant, by the privileged instant of Christ, which the believer must repeat in himself. Thus the instant of plenitude given in Christ sums up, condenses, absorbs everything in itself and removes from the duration which follows it its justification. This does not mean that time does not continue, in appearance, between Jesus and his final advent, nor that the acts of Jesus have not *in fact* results, successions, consequences which unfold in the Church and in the churches. But this means that privileged time, *pure* time, valid time, legitimate time does not exist after the death of the last apostle. Thereafter one cannot find in history an exclusively valid development, as the Roman Catholic Church claims to possess. And, no doubt, the bishops are the "successors" of the apostles, but they are only successors: "after the apostolate," the instant is concluded. There can be a *succession,* but this is not a *continuity.*

It would be easy to find an illustration of this philosophy in the works of Mr. Cullmann on *Christ and Time,* on *Peter,* and on the apostolic tradition.

One could believe that the thought of Mr. Cullmann approaches the Catholic conception since, in opposition to the liberal Protestants and early Barthians, he tends to restore the notion of apostolic tradition, he shows that tradition preceded and conveyed Scripture. One could believe that he grazes the position of Roman Catholics, when in his recent work on *Peter* he accepts the authenticity of the *logion* on the power of the keys (*Tu es Petrus*), when he sees in Peter the head of the apostles and the trustee of the sovereignty—yet without linking this transmission of power to the Vatican at the death of Peter.

But the more the exegesis of Mr. Cullmann approaches the exegesis familiar to Catholics, the better one perceives how different the philosophical substructures are.

Indeed, for Mr. Cullmann, Jesus certainly did transmit the powers to Peter, who is the *rock* upon which Jesus founded his Church. But one does not see that Jesus foresaw or wanted Peter to transmit his power to a successor. And in fact, according to Mr. Cullmann, Peter did not transmit it.

Which amounts to saying that the *Instant of Christ* enlarged: now it includes a first radiation, which is the apostolate, and an apostolate founded on the rock-apostle. But after this radiation, the divine Instant ceases: the Church is not guaranteed, she remains purely human. To found is not to construct. The "foundation" is without real succession: in it the act of founding is exhausted, comes to an end and is limited. The Catholic Church also proclaims the unique character of the Instant of Christ, the privileged character of the second apostolic and papal instant. She admits in the function of the apostles (and of him who is their head) an intransmissible element, *given once and for ever*. But the act of founding the Church, of being "her rock," continues in the successors of Peter on the Roman axis, conceived as indefectible. The Instant LASTS. The duration *is*.

It is not the same for a Protestant type of thought. Kierkegaard expresses the substance of this thought by his concept of Instant and above all by that of Repetition. The Reformers, by withdrawing from the instituted and continuous Church in order to bind themselves to Christ *alone* by grace *alone*, withdrew necessarily from history, and consequently from all metaphysics of historic time. Newman never cited and probably never knew of the Danish thinker, his brother and his opposite. But in the first pages of his *Essay on the Development of Christian Doctrine* he dared to say that Protestantism and history are not in accord: "To be deep in history is to cease to be a Protestant." Let us limit ourselves to remarking that, if one wants to translate the implicit idea of the Reformation on the nature of ecclesial time, one ends up with an ontology of cleavage and discontinuity, with a predominance of the Instant over Duration.

We do not mean that it is necessary to substitute a metaphysics of Duration and of Development for that of the Instant. On the contrary, we believe that whoever wants to envisage *the profound structure* of Christianity must unite in it instant and duration: for the Instant of Christ is indeed the instant of foundation and remains normative in regard to what follows. It is not impossible to think that we will be able to reconcile Kierkegaard and Newman on an elevated plane.[9]

[9] My last discussions with Mr. Cullmann led me to think that our conceptions are drawing closer together. I am more attentive to the consideration of the Instant, as the immediate passage of

Newman did not have his first religious experiences in the High Church: he was not oriented toward the Roman Church by the development of anti-Protestant principles which the High Church had maintained, at the same time as the principles of free enquiry. Much to the contrary, he was led to an inner, living and mystic faith by the evangelical milieu, which was an authentic Calvinism, renewed, *awakened,* made more simple and more interior under the influence of Wesley. And his fundamental idea, expressed as early as the *Lectures on Justification,* is that the *evangelical* faith, if it wants to be not only *durable* but *lasting,* implies the Church and living tradition.

Newman therefore, in his "first conversion," had felt chosen. And he testified in his old age that, even disengaged from the original circumstances and from the dogma of predestination, the experience was just as real. Let us say that there was in him the idea of that vertical instant which, in Christ, continually takes up and repeats itself, like the act of creation.

But Newman, although he put less emphasis on it, goes deeper than Descartes, because he explains duration not by the repetition of the Instant, but by the value of the *Interval.* The fact that the revelation in Christ was made "once for all" (without being able to be understood "all at once"[10]) does not remove from time its value and its

eternity to time. Mr. Cullmann, for his part, admits that there can exist, after Christ and in the Church, privileged manifestations of the Spirit. What he rejects is a normative authority of the Church, which would take the place of that of Scripture (note of 1963).

[10] *Essay,* ch. I, sect. I, §3.

reality: one could say that it establishes it, for *the instant is not the limit, it is the germ of time,* as the infinitesimal element is in calculus. It is thus that the sacraments are continued acts of Christ. It is thus the first moment of the foundation in Peter, the rock, if it keeps its singular value as the origin, is in fact continued by those who do not limit themselves to succeeding the apostles and Peter chronologically, but who represent them and renew them by applying to new circumstances the moment and the intuition of the foundation.

It seems to me that it is not being unfaithful to the mind of Newman to give it these prolongations.

Although Newman always affirmed the discontinuity of spiritual development, which involves sudden beginnings and mutations, which takes place "by fits and starts," with "sudden conversions," he maintains that profound conversion is long, constant, gradual; that we are, so to speak, always called, the call becoming confused with existence; that the waiting of the servant who does not fall asleep is the image of life; that the temporal mixture is not a mosaic of moments of certitude and moments of anxiety, but on the contrary a definite insecurity, involving risks to be victoriously run; that this character of constancy, of continuity, of vigor and of stability, of monochrony and of monotony, if it is often blurred and obscure in the too-brutal cross-section of the present instant, manifests itself peacefully and fully in the operation of the memory;[11] that faith and even reason are not rare acts, improbable up-

[11] See in particular *Parochial Sermons* I, (I); II (X); IV (XVII); VI (I); VIII (XI); VIII (XV) and our work *P.N.*, 29.

heavals, but incarnate faculties, habits of the soul;[12] finally, that these traits which specify human time will continue (less the anxiety) in the purification of purgatory and that thus the states of the *tried life*, the busy time of the earth and the agonizing, radiant time of purgatory, correspond mysteriously to one another—so that death also is but a passage and that after death, spiritual development continues and will never be completed, since eternity will make us further advance "from one degree of splendor to another" (2 Cor 3:18).

In other respects, on a fairly large number of difficulties which nourish the polemics of the separated churches and of the Protestants against the Roman Church, Newman gives the latter the means of diminishing them and of solving them without cheating with the facts, but by illuminating them with a new light, sometimes even by a dialectical inversion, transforming the argument *against* into an argument *for*. Indeed, the principle of the apologetics peculiar to the separated churches is to show their perfect, even in some cases literal, continuity with the doctrines and the practices of the primitive Church. The principle of their refutation of *Roman* Catholicism is to show the additions, superfetations and corruptions introduced by this Church.

And it can be said that Protestantism, by appealing to the *historical method* against the Church, whose metamorphoses it sounded out and then revealed, gave impetus to

[12] *University Sermons*, 36, 37, 101, 104, 172.

that rationalist school of the history of religions, which ranks religions together, which has a tendency to dissolve the originality of the most noble by showing that they are mixtures and mosaics. But Protestantism, sincerely attached to the faith, cannot bear this dissolution of religion by history—whence the obligation in which it finds itself to withdraw from history, either by taking refuge in a philosophy of religion, in the manner of the post-Kantians, or rather, like the Kierkegaardians of our time, by defining the faith by the repetition in it of the Instant of Christ—a sort of cutting into history, inaccessible to the dissolvent operations of criticism which bear only upon duration.

It is here that Newman offers a principle which, by leaving historical documentation in its place, permits the faith to envisage itself without renouncing the study of its own history, but on the contrary, demanding this research.

4

Newman and the Philosophy of Becoming

Let us place ourselves now in a completely different perspective; let us follow from now on a wholly new bent: that of modern thought on *becoming*, of which we have said that it remained of secondary importance in Newman's reflections.

Newman never spoke of Hegel, nor of Spencer, nor of Hegelian *becoming*, nor of Spencerian *evolution*. But if he had known *becoming* and *evolution*, he would have rejected them both.

For Hegel, as for Spencer (that which relates them despite so many differences), integration, instead of being virtually given at the outset in the form of an improbable, initial state which acts as a germ, comes about in the end in the form of a synthesis which includes in it the diversity, the contradiction or the heterogeneity of the antecedent development. It is the future and the final term which is the sole synthesis, that to which the being ascends by successive creations, metamorphoses, which make it have access to a new degree of value.

Since the Second World War, in the most opposed schools of thought, emphasis has been placed on the freedom of man in history. One has rejected the conception of a history which unwinds mechanical, an eternal plan or project, given so to speak in advance, like film before its projection. Stress has been laid on the character which history has of being unforeseeable for us and even of being unforeseeable in itself, because it is produced by the "project" of man. Actually, the conception of an *unfolding history* of intemporal essences is but an imperfect expression of that Eternal—present, creative and simple—in which nothing is predetermined, but in which everything is possessed, everything lives, everything exists. Newman does not obstruct history by reducing it to an unfolding stopped in advance, whose law could be known by human intelligence. Nor does he make of man the demiurge of history, at once exalted and anguished by the power of total creation which is granted him. Newman does not give freedom the power of establishing value, but that of choosing among values which it does not itself place into existence. And, from this point on, the psychic fabric of human time is not woven of pride and anxiety, like the time of the existentialists: it is the time of mingled hope and uneasiness, or rather it is the time of a free security, whose matter is uneasiness. "To be at ease is to be unsafe."[13]

If one wanted to set forth, according to the nature of their hidden reasons, the modern systems concerning "becoming," one would see that they depend on a negative ontological argument, absolutely opposed to that which St. Anselm defined as the nerve and the hidden spring of any proof and even of any idea of God. The ontological argument—which is not a proof of God, but a definition of the mystery hidden in his existence (independently of all creation, revelation or manifestation of this essence, which alone can give rise to a proof)—this argument, I say, is based on the idea that there exists in God alone a necessary relation between his existence and his perfection. Absolute Existence, infinite Perfection are one and the same. Now, any metaphysics of becoming supposes a sort of "*argument néontologique*" (which Jean-Paul Sartre defined, for example, in *Being and Nothingness*): absolute existence and the imperfection of nothingness are one and the same being, for there exists an absurd but necessary relation between "Being" and this "Nothingness," which corrodes it. It would not be necessary to dig very deeply to rediscover this same postulate in all atheism.

The consequence is that no value judgment is justifiable,

[13] *Parochial Sermons*, III (XXV); *Dream of Gerontius*.

since all forms of being, all moments of becoming are modes or phases of this absolute existence, beyond which there is nothing. History becomes the true metaphysics: everything is equally justified.

Newman always supposes, on the contrary, that the plane of the truth transcends the plane of becoming, of history, of essences engaged in time; that consequently *history cannot be the norm or the judge of history, but that there is a judgment of history*. It is an idea which is found already in Platonism, an idea which is imminent to Christian thought, to such a point that we do not realize its presence in us until it is questioned. Taking the adage of Leibniz about the *intellectus* and the *sensus* as a pattern, one could say: "There is nothing in historic becoming which is not historic, if it is not the judgment brought to bear on history itself." What results from this proposition according to which value is not historic in itself, but intemporal and normative in relation to history?

A first consequence is that history is necessarily *plural*. There is not in history, as Hegel and the necessitarians suppose, a *unique* development which absorbs in itself all the others.

But neither does there exist a scattering of historic atoms, of instants without consequence and without posterity, associated randomly like the atoms of Epicurus.

It is thus neither absolute unity nor absolute multiplicity which explains history. But there exists in it, as in all the zones of being, both unity and multiples. If we want to express this view in the language of change, we will say that there exist *developments*, all different, which realize more or less, according to the degrees of participation, their type, their essence, their "Idea."

Therefore, according to the spirit of Newman, when one shows essences in time, one can not fail to ask oneself in what measure that which one has found oneself describing realizes the Idea.[14]

5

Actuality of Newman's Thought

Instant, Becoming, Development: Kierkegaard, Hegel, Newman

Such are the implicit thoughts which define that which could have been the philosophy issued from a Newman turned metaphysician. It is fitting to emphasize once more that Newman never dreamed of defining his thought according to the methods of the philosopher. What is important is that this thought, like that of Socrates, of Pascal or of Kierkegaard, is able to inspire works of philosophy.[15]

[14] Newman rediscovered a conception of history which was related to that with which Husserl was to end up at the end of his career. Husserl said that the ideas, the essences which animate history are not at rest, that they are to no greater extent in the event, but that there is a *genesis of meaning*, an "intentional history"—which the philosopher alone can grasp.

[15] No one has spoken of philosophy with more emotion. He defined it as the exercise of reason in the domain of knowledge. "It is the power of referring every thing to its true place in the universal system, —of understanding the various aspects of each of its parts; —of comprehending the exact value of each, —of tracing each backwards to its beginning, and forward to its end,

"The multitude of men indeed," writes Newman in 1880, "are not consistent, logical, or thorough; they obey no law in the course of their religious views; and while they cannot reason without premisses, and premisses demand first principles, and first principles must ultimately be (in one shape or another) assumptions, they do not recognize what this involves, and are set down at this or that point in the ascending or descending scale of thought, according as their knowledge of facts, prejudices, education, domestic ties, social position, and opportunity for inquiry determine; but nevertheless there is a certain ethical character, one and the same, a system of first principles, sentiments and tastes, a mode of viewing the question and of arguing,

---

—of anticipating the separate tendencies of each, and their respective checks or counteractions; and thus of accounting for anomalies, answering objections, supplying deficiencies, making allowances for errors, and meeting emergencies. It never views any part of the extended subject-matter of knowledge, without recollecting that it is but a part, or without the associations which spring from this recollection. It makes every thing lead to every thing else; it communicates the image of the whole body to every separate member, till the whole becomes in imagination like a spirit, every where pervading and penetrating its component parts, and giving them their one definite meaning. . . . Men, whose minds are possessed by one object, take exaggerated views of its importance, are feverish in their pursuit of it, and are startled or downcast on finding obstacles in the way of it; they are ever in alarm or in transport. . . . But Philosophy cannot be partial, cannot be exclusive, cannot be impetuous, cannot be surprised, cannot fear, cannot lose its balance, cannot be at a loss, cannot but be patient, collected and majestically calm, because it discerns the whole in each part, the end in each beginning, the worth of each interruption, the measure of each delay, because it always knows where it is and how its path lies from one point to another" (*University Sermons*, 291-292).

which is formally and normally, naturally and divinely, the *organum investigandi* given us for gaining religious truth, and which would lead the mind by an infallible succession from the rejection of atheism to theism, and from theism to Christianity, and from Christianity to Evangelical Religion, and from these to Catholicity. And again when a Catholic is seriously wanting in this system of thought, we cannot be surprised if he leaves the Catholic Church, and then in due time gives up religion altogether."[16]

We have tried to show in this study that the thought of Newman is situated between two extreme tendencies, which are in our time subtile temptations for the mind.

It can be said that Newman did not yield either to antihistoric *instantism* or to that historic *totalitarianism* between which, under the sign of Kierkegaard and Hegel, we see modern minds separate. Neither the instant nor becoming can explain history: each of them places us, indeed, outside of and beyond real history, because they substitute for the experience which is in fact given to us, a tracing made by abstract intelligence. If history is reduced to the instant, everything in it which is continuation or interval finds itself deprived of reality. And on the other hand, if all history is conceived as equally given, similarly valid, because necessary, then history—become a concrete logic—cannot give rise to a value judgment. And one must even say that, in this case, history finds itself abolished, since it becomes the scene of a *necessary progress*. On another

[16] Note of 1880, placed in the appendix of the definitive edition of the *Grammar of Assent*. See *P.N.*, xxviii.

plane, one can say that the negation of history, either in the instantist form or in the dialectic form, results in the negation of the Church, which supposes history.

Thus, the philosophy of absolute discontinuity and of the instant, the philosophy of absolute continuity and of integral becoming have the effect of making an intellectual justification of Catholicism impossible. If the Church existed but in the Instant of Jesus, it is necessary to say that since this instant came to an end, she is no longer but a semblance of the Church. And if revelation, conceived as progressive enlightenment, is identified with the universal history of humanity awakening to the consciousness of its intrinsic divinity, then it is necessary to say that the Church has to no greater extent a *raison d'être. Real history and true Church are somehow bound together, in the sense that any justification of the time of the Church finds itself justifying historic time to boot, so to speak, and that inversely any authentic experience of this same historic time is favorable to the understanding of the time peculiar to the Church.* Let us no longer be astonished that Newman, having taken the time of the Church as his subject of study, formed and formulated views on time, history and being that justify them. What is regrettable is that these implicit views have not been made explicit by later disciples. If we designate fairly schematically the two climates of his thought before his conversion to the Catholic climate by the concepts of "Protestantism" and "evolutionism," it can be said that Newman rises above both of them, that he sublimes them and purifies them, rather than that he rejects them in the second period of his life.

These two extremities do not appear on the same plane. Kierkegaard and Newman are fairly closely related. One could even say that Kierkegaard, more Catholic than the Kierkegaardians, advanced on an axis that could have terminated in Newman. *Kierkegaard is opposed to Hegel by essence and to Catholicism only by accident.* The Kierkegaardian instant, that moment in which freedom becomes an act in us, is not an abstract relation isolated in a universe of concepts but an instant which is a germ by the presence in it of freedom. Kierkegaard, contrary to the Greek thinkers or to Hegel, preserves the idea of a possible synthesis of eternity and time, and consequently of the ontological validity of a "people of God," a "sacred history," a "church." His only error in the eyes of a Newmanian would be to be dazzled by the moment of Christ, to set up his tent there, to not admit that the Instant of Christ, the termination of the Jewish period, is developed in a visible Church. On the contrary, Hegel cannot admit a junction of eternity and time: denying transcendence, he can see in eternity and time but two modes of the intemporal, that is to say, two concepts having *connections* between them and not two beings having *relations* between them.

What allows Newman to preserve these values apparently alien to Romanism is the fact that contrary to so many minds, he never gave his experiences an ontological value. Never did he transform them, without meditation and by a conceptual transformation, into philosophical systems. It is rare that those who have known a profound experience, consubstantial with their inner life and above all an "*Erlebnis*" which has marked their life with a cleavage, do not color their entire view of the world with these tints which are peculiar to them. Even an inspired genius like St. Paul, or a theologian of the depths like St. Augustine, have introduced in some way into their speculation terms, formulas, emphases which are only the projection of their singular experience. If one studies a powerful personality like that of Luther, one sees even more clearly, it seems, this projection of the singular, which is experienced, into the universal, which is envisaged. That moderate spirit of Newman, which he owes in part to a long contact with the Greco-Latin tradition, that exceptional virtue of prudence, that sense of the human (which was favored, moreover, by the Anglo-Saxon temperament, in which the overstepping of the limit is rarely exercised) permitted him to make his experience serve the development of his thought, without replacing this thought by a pure and implacable logic.[17]

If we now ask ourselves once more from where Newman drew this virtual doctrine about time, which is the source of his thought, we believe that we can reply that it is from his spiritual experience. The time which he presupposes is not the time of rapture, of ecstasy, of the instant which uproots—and it is to no greater extent the conceptual time of dialectics. Why, then? Because the experience to which Newman refers and which he described with so much finesse and depth in his spiritual works and especially in his *Parochial Sermons*, is the time of the inner life, lived in its duration.

[17] See, regarding these views, *R.N.*, 61-95.

I already alluded to this point a little while ago, but it is necessary to come back to it and to emphasize that there exists in Newman as formally in St. Augustine an analogy between the time of the individual spiritual life and the time of integral history, between the time of the solitary believer and the time of the Church "which is his abode." I said that the characteristic of this inner time was its continuity along the line where the self develops, matures and in some way is pre-eternized, although remaining subject to vigilance, to risk and to uneasiness. From this point of view, this time is fairly different from that which St. Augustine describes in the *Confessions,* which is a time essentially divided in two, according as it disperses into sin or collects itself in the movement of conversion, a time which St. Augustine finds again on the macrocosmic scale in the *City of God,* in which he depicts an inexpiable struggle between two currents. Newmanian time does not bring about any crisis, for it is a perpetual crisis. It absorbs in itself crisis and division. It does not present the privileged moment of freedom or of grace, but it is in its entirety freedom and grace. And, to take another point of comparison in order to make the originality of this Newmanian time stand out, I remark that it has but distant resemblances with Bergson's duration, because in Bergson time is above all the scene of freedom conceived and experienced as a power of invention, of unforeseeableness. One cannot say that Newman is in the least sensible to this creative and continually regenerating aspect of spiritual time: on the contrary, in Newman time would be rather the time of permanence and even of a certain monotony—at the limit, of a perpetual recommencement, of a certain tedium or rather of a "habit of the soul." If one wanted to define that which is peculiar to this time of Newman, I believe that it would be necessary to have recourse to an aspect which it always supposes: that of a slow, gradual, progressive, almost imperceptible development. The word which seems to me here the least inexact would be "maturation."

And it is certainly also a matter of *maturation* in the life of the Church: we see the *same*, being carried on through *the other*, but in such a way that this *same* remains the *same*, although under varied and ever more comprehensive forms. Newman did not perhaps explicitly insist upon this recapitulating and "involving" aspect of time which, as it advances (like the memory), collects, takes up again, integrates in itself the completed duration and thus becomes accumulated past. Newman was not sensitive to everything with which eschatology provides us, which is to make us sensitive to the recapitulating and "*ana cephalaiotic*" moment in which everything will be reduced to a single point, as to a head, to a final and definitive *sum*. Newman lived in an age of progress and hope in which humanity was more appreciative of "evolution" than of "involution." But when one looks more closely and above all when one considers his thoughts on "development" in their last phase at the end of his life, one sees that he put more emphasis then on permanence than on growth. Time, as it advanced, seemed to him to conserve itself, to be equivalent to itself, rather than to change or even to progress or to grow.

And I would be inclined to believe that it is the recourse to human experience which permitted him to escape systematization.

One sees him avoid the *passage to the extreme* which carries away in general the historian-philosophers of his time. Never does he substitute for history a *law* of development, an immanent *dialectic*. Never does he even rewrite a *Discourse on Universal History*. Although, like any mind nourished on the Bible, he believes profoundly in a Providence which acts upon history, one does not see him determine the law of this providential action, nor even try to justify it, be it in its main lines. There would rather be in Newman a pessimistic view of history, leading him to think that history is the reign of competitions among parties, of degradations of these parties, the scene of a general obscuring of everything: the sole exception would be an axis, a spring on which the great individualities would come to cling at intervals. In a more general way, let us say that Newman, although he admits a divine plane and a counsel of God, does not raise himself up to this plane and to this counsel. Nor does one sense in him to a greater extent the optimism of Leibniz. He does not maintain that the conduct of God is regulated by a "principle of the best," which we would be able to know and of which we would even be able to deduce the particularity of beings and the concatenation of circumstances.

That which relates St. Augustine and Newman is the fact that they perceived a coincidence between their solitary history and universal history. The experience of a creative intimacy, felt through the events of their own history, led them to discover in human history the presence of this same intimacy—the Catholic Church having in this universal history of humanity the role which the consciousness of the self assumes in the individual life.

And one could say that Newman's existential experience better disposed him to the understanding of divine history than that of St. Augustine. The latter did not know the extremely mild deepenings brought by the continuous passage from an imperfect enlightenment to total enlightenment which gave Newman the full sense of the development of the Church.

Christianity alone is capable of giving the key of both these worlds, the interior world and the historic world, of showing how they accord, rely on and correspond to one another. The idea which unfolds in the *City of God* had animated the intellectual and political civilization of the Middle Ages; it had become anemic and impoverished, to disappear at that critical instant when humanity, by splitting up into nations, divided against itself. The success of the Reformation had kept it from being restored under a form suited to new times. One can say that it was missing in the seventeenth century; it is its absence which makes for the infirmity of Descartes despite so much greatness. It is its presence which, despite so much weakness, makes for the interest of positivism. In order to support its great works, the nineteenth century needed to rediscover this ancient view. This view was given to it by Hegel under a logical, precarious and erroneous form. The thought of

Newman was capable of being that development of Augustinianism which our century needs. Hegel was listened to, Newman ignored. Hegel has been able to be called the master of contemporary scholasticism. Newman had no echo. If he had created a school, one would have seen develop a psychology of implicit thought and profound life, a logic of conviction, a sociology of Idea and influence, a theology at once dogmatic, psychological and positive, a mystics of the Church, a veritable temporal-eternal. The philosophies which rest in the accustomed divisions, those which fascinate by subtile novelties, are assured of a more general success.

Newman would hardly accept the epithet of *current*, which is humiliating. What chance exists, indeed, for the mode, that extremely momentary unanimity, to approach the integral truth? Why give to the present such a privilege? There is not an atom of modernism in Newman. But one can love one's time and be sensitive to the aspect of eternal truth which it manifests to us. Vauvenargues said: "It is for lack of penetration that we reconcile so few things." Newman had this penetration. And that is why he will deserve perhaps one day to be honored with that glorious name of "father," which the Church reserves to those who have preadapted it.[18]

[18] A shrewd observer, who in 1867 described philosophy in France in the nineteenth century, consecrated several lines to Newman, even though he was a foreigner. He pronounced this prophetic judgment, which was commendable at this date of 1867: "A time will come perhaps before long in which the idea of development will prevail in religion, no less than in any science; such,

May I cite here that wish once culled from the mouth of Pius XII: "Newman will one day be a doctor of the Church."

---

for example, as the eminent Catholic doctor, Mr. Newman, has set it forth, an idea which wins over more minds from day to day. At this time a broader doctrine of interpretation will be established. Freer, theology will get still more use from philosophy and will also render it more services. And it is then that one will be able to see finally come true that great saying of St. Augustine, that true religion and true philosophy do not differ" (Ravaisson, *La Philosophie en France au XIXe siècle*, Paris 1867, 154.

Conclusion

The Church, the Axis of History

I would like to *think* the Church. And for that, I contemplate, imitating the geometricians, proceeding by definitions. I am going to go from the exterior—that is, from appearances—toward the interior—that is, toward the real intimity.

At each stage of this examination, I will probably see certain friends detach themselves from me; I will probably be ever more abandoned and finally I will remain almost solitary in the midst of men with—alone—the faithful of Roman Catholicism. In order to pass from one level of knowledge to the superior level, it will be necessary for me to demand a new effort of vision, of transparence and of ascension, a *conversion*. The advantage will be that by rising from stage to stage, I will enter more and more into the savor, into the depth of unfathomable eternity.

Here is the first definition which I propose to myself:

In one of the innumerable galaxies, on one planet of the solar system inhabited by life, sustaining therefore thought and love, Catholicism is the form of religion the most capable of extending itself, without being divided, in space and time. It presents itself as the work of a Founder called Jesus, conceived as sent by God.

This is a description of appearances, to which the pure historian can hold.

I think it is necessary to keep it in mind in order to enlarge Catholicism to all the dimensions of the universe. We have now come to a time in which we are forced to think the entire *cosmos*, to envisage the universe. Is the *roseau pensant* limited to man? We must admit the possibility of the plurality of worlds. And there will perhaps be for our descendants a moment when they will be led to enter into contact with another type of reasonable beings. What will then become of the Church?

Either these reasonable beings will not know Jesus, or else the Word will have been incarnate, adapted, communicated in another form among them. In the latter case, there can no more be two churches than there are two reasons. The terms of this other Church should have their correspondence in our language. There would be, for the truths of faith as for those of science and of reason, a transposition to make by the play of analogy, as when we discover an unknown language, for the identity of faith with faith recalls, on its level, the identity of reason with reason.

The linking of worlds inhabited by the Spirit cannot take place but in their Source and their Cause, that is, in God. He alone can found the union of spirits incarnate, disincarnate, or nonincarnate, as are the angels, whose existence is assured by revelation.

Nothing forbids thinking that the religion revealed to this planet is the religion of all the humanities, real or possible. Certain prayers of Catholic worship, like the common preface, in which the celebrant appeals to the celestial choirs; certain sealed books like the Apocalypse lead one to think that the Catholic Church is as vast as the worlds of the universe, that she possesses in herself a principle capable of extending itself to the All.

I leave this plane of the cosmos and of appearances of space and time in order to go to the causes. I take for granted the faith in Jesus, Son of God and Savior. I then obtain a second definition of Catholicism.

In *catholic,* I have said, there is *universe.* Catholic, in a sense, means: *Beyond.* Beyond any race, any nation; beyond any system, any limit; beyond everything which could restrict a truth.

How difficult it is to be equal to this exigency and to bear worthily this name of Catholic! For the *catholic* element is never disincarnate, uprooted, without color, or face, or visage. Quite to the contrary, everything which is catholic is seen to have sent down roots.

The first Catholics were Jews with a Judaic horizon. Their successors were Greeks who thought like Greeks. Then they were Romans. And the Church took the colors of the Roman majesty. In each nation, she singularized herself. There was an Alexandrian Church, a Church of Antioch, a Frankish Church . . . Anyone will be able to go on. And he will observe that there are many ways of being Catholic. But then, one measures the difficulty of being it well, since, while accepting one's own roots and one's own colors, it is necessary to distinguish them from Catholicism which is universal and which accommodates itself also to other kind of roots. One can imagine that the temptation is great, for a mind born Catholic, to confuse his manner of being with his being and to want to propose his habits to the universe of consciences.

For a religion to be universal, it needs a center of unity, a single faith, a supreme authority. But it is also necessary for this religion to be such that it can receive in it and gather into its unity all human diversities. It is necessary that there be but one flock and one Shepherd, but it is also necessary that the sheepfold be able to contain all the sheep. And it is supremely desirable that one day these sheep hear the voice of the one Shepherd and find themselves all under his staff with their particular varieties, with all their own colors, and if I dare say, their singular bleatings.

To translate the same idea, I propose this formula to myself:

The Church is the form of history, that is to say, the instigating organ, which would permit each historic existence to grow in conformity with its own essence.

Externally, the Church can seem to be but an adventitious and antiquated construction, a château once fortified which is crumbling away under the effect of the centuries. It has always been in the destiny of the Church to thus appear a superfetation, a sort of thing which is *always de trop*, like existence, like death. In the beginnings, Marcus Aurelius considered the little Christianity a tumor which it would be necessary to cut out. In our era, some would like also to operate upon this widespread cancer, these Catholic pustules which are suppurating. So the world sees with its terrestrial regard.

These appearances, so manifestly contrary to the profound reality, are due to the fact that one considers but a single aspect of the problem, that one sees but a single point and not all the points, at once in the ensemble and in the ensembles. If one looked with a profound, inner and total regard, one would perceive that the Church is the *form* of the All. She is ready to give form to whatever occurs in the domain of the mind or of history, that is, to keep it from becoming corrupt, to make it develop. Be it a matter of Scriptures or of prophecies, of theological doctrines or of mystical states, of realms or of social movements, of antiquities, of renaissances, of novelties of culture and of civilization, the Church can assume them by letting them be what they are, by giving them merely a pure destination, which would be their true destiny.

There are but the "reforms" made with violence or with trickery against her essence that she cannot assume: she is then forced to point them out and to let them go to their fate of separation. She no longer assumes the responsibility for them. She commits them to the laws of the world; laws of temporary growth, of tumescence, of inward division and of putrefaction. As for her, by grace and by surprise as by hope, she escapes these laws: that is a strength which is peculiar to her. One is quite conscious (and that is why she calls herself "catholic," she has so much confidence!) that she has the power of doing full justice to that which exists, of respecting it and vivifying it, of incarnating it to a greater extent "according to its species," of restoring that which exists to its own manner of existing. I say that she has this power. I do not say that she exercises it always and necessarily, with equity, with wisdom, felicitously, nor that Catholics are all capable or worthy of such a demanding vocation. But I am considering the Catholic phenomenon in its broadest extensions and in its longest durations.

It is necessary to judge a universal institution on the scale of universal history, and not by those snapshot cross-sections which, generally, show only what is unaccomplished or what is faltering. But the Church *informs* all human time, that time whose unit of measure is perhaps the space of three centuries. She has lived several of these periods of three hundred years, which measure in religion the maximal duration of a dominion of ideas.

: : :

If thus I consider the Church in time by reading her history on a long scale, I see her identical to herself, dominating the men, the conjunctures, the problems—which flow by in her and which leave her unchanged. The idea which we have of a permanent institution, identical to itself, which would dominate the flow of time, which would be really *abode*—it is the Church which realizes it the least imperfectly. One was less conscious of it, probably, in the

Middle Ages, when political institutions seemed eternal and by divine right. But it was the Catholic Church which gave this "divine right."

She is the true *abode* of those demanding and solitary minds, who loath being conformists and who yet want to be in harmony with the rest of mankind. She is the *abode* of all the things which want to be linked with the rest of the things, to survive beyond the furtive instant. Despite appearances, in the societies of our time one has hardly any freedom, it is necessary to conform, and nonconformism is a rather harsh tyrant for the young. The sites of pleasures are the most regulated and the most dismal of places. Outside of one's house, one has no freedom, one cannot even change the disposition of objects. The Church is a house of many mansions, *an abode of abodes*, where each one can silently build his freedom without fearing the excesses of this freedom, for his freedom finds itself harmonized with all the others, and consequently linked, coordinated, wisely necessitated.

And one can not make history but from that which abides or from that which causes to abide.

The Church performs, for the body of humanity itinerant in time, that function of permanence which the conscience, the memory, the "self" of the depths, by whatever name one calls them, perform in the life of the individual. And it is not (for me, at least) a surprise that the authors who, from tens of centuries to tens of centuries, have best spoken of the Church, St. Augustine and Newman, have also been *autobiographers*.

Having the inner eye trained on their tragic and sublime history, concerned about discerning the permanence of their innermost being through vicissitudes, having profoundly changed in order *to remain the same*, St. Augustine and Newman were capable of understanding that solid Catholic Church to which they arrived in the middle of their life, which was for them a Mother according to the spirit, a milieu favorable for unceasing progress in confidence. Universal history with the Church at the center was in reality, for them, two aspects of one and the same problem always resolved: *permanence in diversity*. Let change, and as one says nowadays, *becoming*, be! But at the interior of a unity more profound than it, of something which anticipates and which recapitulates, which is still more present than the present.

: : :

The two definitions which I gave kept us still on a visible and temporal place. They do not make us penetrate into the secret of divine life on earth. I would like to try to go beyond them. And I propose this third definition:

Catholicism is the name given in human history to the Mystical Body of Christ, that is, to that communion of consciences united to Christ by the bond of love, according to their ever growing capacity, and into whom flows the grace of a participation in divine life.

Catholicism is the mystery of eternity already present in time through its germs.

This definition demands a further advancement in faith.

At the dawn of Christian times, this advancement characterizes the Gospel of St. John in relation to the first three Gospels. The first three, indeed, had started from time, whereas the fourth starts from eternity. The events and the characters are the same: the lighting differs. The light, in the last Gospel, comes from above. It descends. It does not ascend. Time is not an absolute point of departure but for those who are subjected to it. The circuit of the real starts from eternity to come to eternity or, as St. John puts it, it goes from the Father to the Father.

Unlike communist society which, according to the logic of atheism, occupies but time, and which believes itself capable of organizing it, even of stopping it at the moment of bliss, the visible Church considers herself transitory. She proclaims that she is in a *militant* state, preparatory to a *triumphant* state; but, at that time, she sees herself outside of time. In this sense, militant Catholicism represents an interval, an interim regime, bound to temporal existence. "Adieu, Holy Catholic Church," Bossuet has the dying man to whom he ministers say. And Newman noted that the seer of the Apocalypse does not see any temples in heaven.

Faith consists in seeing Jesus existing in this very moment, although invisible, but with a presence superior to that which we call, here below, "presence," which is above all the occupancy of a location: and what is location? The presence of the historic Jesus extended but to a small group of companions in a fragment of space and time. This presence extends now to the universe of consciences which believe in him. By the visible Church, which is a sort of "body of Christ," this presence penetrates almost all the elements of the human community which, consciously or unconsciously, are now touched by uneasiness and, in a certain sense, *evangelized*. To be sure, many of these elements are alien, ignorant, mortally hostile: but what is happening in the profound consciousness, where the radical freedom of man is situated?

By placing oneself into historic experience, by comparing the diverse civilizations, one can ascertain that Jesus is the sole being known who presents such a prolongation. By a retrospective effect, made possible by the existence of prophecies, Jesus succeeded in *being* before existing: being announced, foretold and, if one can say it, fore-lived by a people and several privileged persons. This is a phenomenon unique of its kind and which can be explained but in two ways: by a mythical illusion or by the person of Jesus being a supreme Existent, "the greatest existent of the earth," if one measures the existence of a being by its dwelling in consciences and by the loves which it arouses. This super-existence constitutes the mystical reality of the Church.

DATE DUE

JY 19 '67			
OC 2 4 '67			
JY 5 '68			
JA 24 '69			
AP 1 9 '69			
JY 12 '69			
AP 27 '71			
GAYLORD			PRINTED IN U.S.A.